LEARNING

LLOYD R. PETERSON

Indiana University

Scott, Foresman and Company • Glenview, Illinois

Dallas, Tex. • Oakland, N.J. • Palo Alto, Cal. • Tucker, Ga. • Brighton, England

Library of Congress Catalog Card Number: 74-82300
ISBN: 0-673-05050-5

ACKNOWLEDGMENTS

The author and publisher wish to thank the following authors and publishers for permission to reproduce or redraw the figures on the following pages: p. 4, Schneiderman, N., Fuentes, I., and Gormezano, I., "Acquisition and extinction of the classically conditioned eyelid response in the albino rabbit," *Science,* 1962, *136,* 651. Copyright © 1962 by the American Association for the Advancement of Science.   p. 6, Kimble, G. A., and Reynolds, B., "Eyelid conditioning as a function of the interval between conditioned and unconditioned stimuli." In G. A. Kimble (Ed.), *Foundations of conditioning and learning.* New York: Appleton-Century-Crofts, 1967, p. 284. Copyright © 1967 by Appleton-Century-Crofts and the American Psychological Association and reprinted by permission.   p. 8, Hartman, T. F., and Grant, D. A., "Effect of intermittent reinforcement on acquisition, extinction, and spontaneous recovery of the conditioned eyelid response," *Journal of Experimental Psychology,* 1960, *60,* 90. Copyright © 1960 by the American Psychological Association and reprinted by permission.   p. 10, Taylor, J. A., "The relationship of anxiety to the conditioned eyelid response," *Journal of Experimental Psychology,* 1951, *41,* 88. Copyright © 1951 by the American Psychological Association and reprinted by permission.   p. 18, Azrin, N. H., and Holz, W. C., "Punishment." In W. K. Honig, *Operant behavior.* New York: Appleton-Century-Crofts, 1966, p. 404. Based on data from Herman, R. L., and Azrin, N. H., "Punishment by noise in an alternative response situation," *Journal of the Experimental Analysis of Behavior,* 1964, *7,* 185–188. Copyright © 1966 by Appleton-Century-Crofts and reprinted by permission.   p. 32, Spence, K. W., "The differential response in animals to stimuli varying within a single dimension," *Psychological Review,* 1937, *44,* 433.   p. 33, Terrace, H. S., "Wavelength generalization after discrimination with and without errors," *Science,* 1964, *144,* 79.   pp. 36–38, Harlow, H. F., "The formation of learning sets," *Psychological Review,* 1949, *56,* 53,

Foreword

Both the content and the format of the beginning course in psychology vary widely today, not only between institutions and departments but also between instructors within the same department. There is a range of acceptable possibilities for organizing the course and considerable freedom for the instructor to select and emphasize those aspects of modern psychology which he considers most important and useful. One of the major reasons for course differences is the variety of subject matter and topics that are grouped under psychology. It is impossible to give adequate treatment to all the relevant topics within the time limitations typically imposed on the introductory course. To make matters more complicated, the accumulation of knowledge is proceeding at such a rapid pace in the different areas of psychology that it is virtually impossible for anyone to keep pace with new developments in all these fields. Thus, an instructor often rightfully limits his treatment to those topics which he feels competent to present with knowledge and understanding. Finally, the current emphasis, in response largely to student and public demand, on the uses of psychology, on its relevance, must be noted. To be sure, not all instructors are convinced of the appropriateness of teaching the application of psychology in the beginning course, pointing to the potential dangers of a little knowledge and of premature attempts to use information not well tested or standardized. In contrast, however, many who teach the introductory course give considerable time and attention to the application and the meaning of what is known.

With this variety in content, technique, and orientation among instructors, there is need for a corresponding variety of textual material. The Scott, Foresman Basic Psychological Concepts Series has been prepared in response to that need. Each title within the Series addresses a single topic. While the volumes are relatively brief, each gives a more intensified development of the topic than is available in any omnibus introductory textbook. Each volume has been prepared by an expert, who presents not only full knowledge of the current substantive and methodological state of his field, but who also provides an original and creative treatment of this material. The books are more than the typical cut-and-dried survey of a topic. There is room in each for the kind of original analysis of the problem heretofore unavailable in introductory reading.

Each title in the Series is independent of the others. They all have been written as a whole so as to maximize the coverage of psychology with minimal overlap and redundancy. No single title is a prerequisite to any other in the Series. At the same time, we should note that there is considerable cross-referencing among the volumes and a general attempt at integrating facts and theories that are pertinent to several topics. While the titles are independent and may be used alone, they are also part of a larger, coordinated, comprehensive survey and interpretation of psychology.

The purpose of the Series is to provide both flexibility and expertise for the instructor and the student in the beginning course. The Series is adaptable to a variety of educational goals. The teacher can select and construct a set of reading units, with the content, emphasis, and sequence he desires, that will fit the general purpose and orientation of this course. He may, for example, base his course on several selected topics, each of which is developed in a separate volume. Alternatively, he might use only a single volume to fill a void or to further develop a topic of special importance. Volumes from the Series may be used in conjunction with most general textbooks. It is furthermore conceivable that one or another of the volumes would be useful in advanced courses, as preliminary reading for the student ill-prepared to contend with a topic on that level or as a supplement developing the background in a related topic. Because of the distinguished authorship of this Series, the teacher can feel confident in his selection without fear of uneven quality, superficiality, or duplication. This Series has a variety of uses at different educational levels, depending upon the needs of the student, the purpose of the course, and the creativity and imagination of the instructor.

In *Learning,* Lloyd Peterson takes a broad and complex topic and presents it in a cogent and straightforward manner. His book simplifies this comprehensive topic without sacrificing significant information. Peterson strives for understanding and his approach is refreshingly clear. In our view, it is the best introductory treatment of learning that has yet been written. No significant facet of the topic is omitted, and yet the reader is not overwhelmed. We believe that both students and teachers will find reading this book a rewarding and informative experience.

Learning is the most basic and most complex of all psychological processes. If an organism could not learn, it would be doomed to repeat only those behaviors which are innate or inborn. The ability to learn is what separates animals from other forms of life, though, of course, the learning of which a particular animal is capable depends upon its species, neurological equipment, and other biological considerations. It is learning that allows us to adapt, within relatively brief periods of time, to the requirements of our circumstances. It is by means of learning that information about our environment gets into our minds and becomes available for use both now and in the future. For human beings, learning is the basis of just about all behavior. It shapes our motives and our emotions. It provides the background for thought. It determines our social activities. It gives rise to our personalities.

Learning has been a topic of primary interest throughout the history of psychology. Psychology's view of learning has changed dramatically over the years. The earliest theories were largely associationistic, holding that events which entered the mind were associated with one another on the basis of contiguity of occurrence, similarity, and certain other principles. During the behaviorist revolution in psychology, learning came to be viewed exclusively as a particular kind of change in overt performance. The basic principles were those of conditioning, especially classical conditioning. A person learned to respond (R) in a particular way in each stimulus situation (S) that he encountered. The stimulus situation controlled his overt behavior. Behavior was a matter of S-R connections formed through conditioning. Associationistic and conditioning analyses, while obviously valuable, have been superseded in part by more recent ideas about the human organism as an information-processing system. Still, information-processing operations, like associations and S-R units, must have some means of entering the mind. Modern theorists agree with their historical counterparts in emphasizing learning as the basis for the development of these operations.

Lyle E. Bourne, Jr., Series Editor, University of Colorado
Leonard Berkowitz, Series Editor, University of Wisconsin

Preface

This book surveys classical as well as contemporary experimental approaches to the study of learning. Specific learning tasks are considered in order of increasing complexity, beginning with conditioning and continuing with tasks requiring information processing of higher degrees of organization. Some contemporary theoretical formulations are examined as examples of the highest level of learned activity—creative thinking.

The primary emphasis here is on ways in which psychologists discover and test principles involved in learning. Readers are invited to discover for themselves application of learning principles to their academic study, their performance of motor skills, and their problem-solving behavior. Examples are provided which will hopefully lead to appreciation of the relevance of learning to related areas of psychology such as motivation and emotion, social interaction, and maladaptive behavior.

I am indebted to Margaret Jean Peterson and Eliot Hearst, colleagues at Indiana University, for helpful comments after reading portions of early drafts of the book. Joanne Elliott has provided editorial expertise which influenced the final version.

Lloyd R. Peterson
Bloomington, Indiana

Table of Contents

INTRODUCTION *1*

1
CLASSICAL CONDITIONING *3*

Anticipation *3*
Types of Responses *5*
Interstimulus Interval *5*
Extinction *7*
Partial Reinforcement *7*
Generalization and Discrimination *8*
Higher-order Conditioning *9*
Individual Differences *9*
Interpretation *10*

2
INSTRUMENTAL CONDITIONING *13*

Reinforcement in Instrumental Conditioning *14*
  Shaping *14*
  Chaining *14*
  Schedules of Reinforcement *15*
Extinction *16*
Conditioned Reinforcers *16*
  Discrimination and Generalization *17*
Punishment *18*
Avoidance and Escape Training *19*
Applications of Conditioning Principles *20*
  Interactions of Classical and Instrumental Conditioning *20*
  Instrumental Conditioning of Autonomic Responses *20*
  Modification of Problem Behavior *21*
  Aversion Therapy *23*

3

THE CONCEPT OF REINFORCEMENT 24

The Basic Element in Reinforcement 24
    Drive Reduction 24
    Onset of Stimulation 24
    Activity Rate 26
Is Reinforcement Necessary for Learning? 26
    Latent Learning and Extinction 27
    Auto-shaping 27
Incentive Motivation 28
Information 29
Awareness 29

4

LEARNING TO DISCRIMINATE 31

A Continuity Interpretation 31
    Summation of Excitation and Inhibition 31
    Peak Shift 32
    Transposition 33
A Noncontinuity Interpretation 34
    Hypothesis Testing 34
    Reversal of Cues 34
    Overtraining 35
Learning to Learn 35
    Object Discrimination 35
    Discrimination Reversals 37
    Dimensional Shifts 38
    Selective Attention 40
Perceptual Learning 42
    Distinctive Features 42
    Coding Responses 42
    Complex Perception 44
    Sensory Substitution 45

5

VERBAL LEARNING 46

Characteristics of Verbal Items 47
    Meaningfulness 47
    Imagery Value 48
Free-recall Learning 49
    Subjective Organization 49
    Part-whole Transfer 50
    Hierarchical Organization 51

Paired-associate Learning   *52*
   Associative Component   *52*
   Response Learning   *54*
   Stimulus Learning   *55*
   Transfer Effects   *55*
Serial Learning   *57*
   Effective Stimulus   *57*
   Grammatical Structure   *58*

6
RETENTION   *60*

Information Processing   *61*
   Sensory Memory   *62*
   Working Memory   *63*
   Long-term Memory   *66*
   Incidental Versus Instructed Learning   *68*
Interference and Forgetting   *69*
   Retroactive Interference   *70*
   Proactive Interference   *73*
   Decay Versus Interference   *76*

7
SKILLED PERFORMANCE   *79*

Stages in Acquisition of Skill   *79*
   Early Stage   *79*
   Intermediate Stage   *80*
   Late Stage   *82*
   Limit   *83*
The Role of Feedback   *86*
   Intrinsic Feedback   *86*
   Augmented Feedback   *86*
Central Factors   *89*
   Internal Standards   *89*
   Motor Programs   *90*
   Organization   *91*
Conditions of Practice   *92*
   Distribution of Practice   *92*
   Part Versus Whole   *94*

8
THINKING   *95*

Representation   *95*
   Animal Representation   *95*
   Human Representation   *96*

Concept Learning *97*
  Attribute Identification *97*
  Rule Learning *98*
Problem Solving *99*
  Hypothesis Testing *100*
  Strategies *101*
  Functional Fixedness *102*
  Subgoals *103*
Game Playing *104*
  Planning Ahead *105*
  Learning to Play *105*

9
INTERPRETATIONS OF LEARNING *107*

Abstraction *107*
Conditioning Theories *108*
Information Processing *110*
Computer Simulation *112*
Mathematical Models *115*
Concluding Remarks *118*

REFERENCES *119*

NAME INDEX *130*

SUBJECT INDEX *132*

Introduction

Everyday living is filled with knowledge, skills, and interests which are mainly the products of past experience. Most individuals in our culture learn to speak, read, and write, but these language skills are only part of what is learned. We acquire complex motor skills as in driving an automobile, or skiing. We learn to react emotionally, so that some fear those who administer punishment, and others become ill when faced with an unpleasant task.

Granted that learning influences almost everything we do, a distinction should be made between our activity and the learning that made it possible. The term *learning* is a scientific construct based on observations of behavior in repeated situations. If we observe athletes early in their careers and again some years later, we note a difference in performance and infer that the difference is due to learning. When we observe improving reading accuracy in children from week to week, we infer that learning is taking place. Thus, learning or lack of it is *inferred* from both observation of performance and the situation evoking the performance. As such, we may define learning as the relatively permanent changes in the potential for performance that result from our interactions with the environment. Temporary changes due to fatigue or drugs are excluded.

If we consider the question of whether any of our behavior is free from the influence of learning, we find there are a few built-in responses to environmental stimulation. These simple behaviors or *reflexes* appear in human beings as well as other organisms. One example is the jerk of the leg when the tendon over the knee is tapped; another is the closure of the eyelid when a puff of air hits the cornea. In contrast, there are complicated sequences of actions carried out over substantial periods of time that are referred to as instinctive behavior.

In some species fairly complex sequences of actions may occur in virtually the same way for every animal of the species apart from any apparent opportunity for learning. For instance, Eibl-Eibesfeldt (1967) described stereotyped behavior of squirrels that is appropriately called *instinctive.* Squirrels scratch a hole with their forepaws, deposit a nut, hammer it into the ground with the snout, sweep earth over the nut with their paws, and stamp the earth down. Another example is mating activity and maternal behavior that seems to be largely unlearned in many animals. Closer investigation may show that some examples of apparently instinctive behavior do involve learning, but there are cases where animals show sequences of unlearned behavior.

There was a time when a great deal of explanation in psychology consisted of calling behavior instinctive. Individuals fought because they were aggressive by nature; they gathered in groups because they were instinctively gregarious. At the present time, few psychologists use instinct as an explanatory factor, at least in the case of humans. We do not exhibit the detailed, stereotyped, unlearned behaviors that some lower animals show; for instance, human beings must learn to care for their young. It is impossible to explain human behavior by referring simply to instincts.

When one is said to have behaved instinctively, this description usually refers to a quick reaction enacted without thinking through alternatives. This kind of action frequently involves a learned *skill,* and it is not accurately described as instinctive behavior or an unlearned reaction. The behavior of an automobile driver in an emergency depends on skills which have been practiced for months and years. While the reaction occurs without thinking, past experiences determine the action; highly practiced skills run off quickly and automatically. In this respect skills resemble reflexes, but skills are the end result of many learning experiences, whereas reflexes are unlearned.

Automatic responding is not the only product of learning. We also learn to solve problems and apply principles from past learning to new learning. Thus, we learn to stop and think when appropriate. So we return to the theme that learning influences most of the activity that constitutes daily living. It makes possible skilled, automatic performance as well as deliberative thought. Even reflexive behavior can be made the basis for learning, as will be discussed in Chapter 1.

1

Classical Conditioning

ANTICIPATION

An elementary type of learning can be readily demonstrated with an infant. Let the baby see your hand at some distance, and then slowly bring your hand closer until you gently tickle the baby's ribs and laughter results. After a few repetitions of this sequence, the baby will begin to smile at the sight of your approaching hand. This type of learning is called classical conditioning. If we analyze this example, we can identify two classes of stimuli, energy changes acting on the child's senses, and the responses which are defined in terms of their related stimuli. The laughing in response to the tickling is called an unconditioned response (UCR); it is behavior produced by the unconditioned stimulus (UCS), the contact with the ribs. This stimulus-response relationship could be observed at the beginning of the demonstration. A second stimulus-response relationship was learned during the course of the demonstration; a conditioned stimulus (CS), the sight of the hand, and a conditioned response (CR), the anticipatory smile at the sight of the approaching hand.

In general, classical conditioning builds upon a stimulus-response relationship, often a reflex, which can be observed prior to the conditioning session. The unconditioned stimulus (UCS) is presented together with another stimulus which does not elicit a response like that of the unconditioned response (UCR). This second stimulus, which initially does not evoke the unconditioned response (UCR), becomes the conditioned stimulus (CS). After presentation of the UCS and the CS at about the same time on a number of occasions or trials, the CS acquires a tendency to evoke a response similar to the UCR, and this response is called the conditioned response (CR).

The systematic investigation of conditioning was initiated by Ivan Pavlov, a Russian psychologist. In the process of studying the digestive processes of dogs, he observed that the dogs salivated when they heard the footsteps of the person who customarily fed them. Since the saliva flowed before the dogs even saw the food, Pavlov concluded this was a psychological process, in contrast to a physiological process such as digestion. Pavlov proceeded to study this anticipatory responding with the same zeal that won him a Nobel Prize for the study of digestion. While Pavlov was not the first to observe anticipatory responding in animals, his contribution was to devise techniques to measure and control the process in the laboratory, and to introduce some concepts which are still in use.

Pavlov's objective in studying anticipation was that of scientists in general: to discover regularities in the processes under observation. The discovery of laws requires precise techniques for measuring various aspects of the process, and these Pavlov imported from physiology. Something more readily controlled than footsteps was needed as a CS, so the ticking of a metronome was used. Measurement of the amount of salivation was made possible by introducing a tube into the dog's mouth and leading the saliva off to a receptacle.

The results of an animal conditioning experiment (Schneiderman, Fuentes, & Gormezano, 1962) are graphed in Figure 1. Rabbits were conditioned to blink their eyes whenever a tone sounded. The UCS was a puff of air to the cornea of the eye. The tone sounded half a second before the onset of the airpuff, and if a rabbit blinked during this interval the blink was counted as a CR. Each animal received eighty-two learning

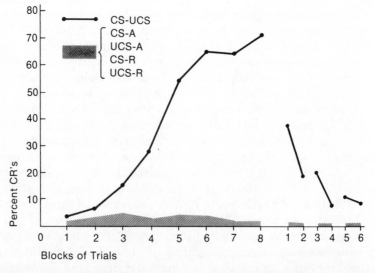

FIGURE 1 Classical conditioning of the eye blink in rabbits. Mean percentages of anticipatory blinks are plotted in 82 trial blocks during conditioning and in 41 trial blocks on three succeeding days when the UCS was omitted. The shaded area at the bottom represents control animals for whom the CS or UCS either occurred alone (A) on each trial, or both occurred at random (R) times. Anticipatory blinks in control animals did not exceed 5 percent.

trials per day for eight days, and the percentage of anticipatory blinks rose steadily during that period. Starting with the ninth day, the UCS no longer followed the tone, and the percentage of blinks to the tone quickly decreased.

TYPES OF RESPONSES

One significant aspect of classical conditioning is that it may involve responses not normally under voluntary control. One does not ask a person to salivate and expect compliance, and yet salivation, digestion, heart rate, and similar responses of humans and other animals can be influenced through conditioning. Our internal body processes are affected by our experiences, and malfunctioning may be brought on by the stimulus situation in which we find ourselves.

In addition, research shows that complex response patterns related to emotions can be conditioned. In a well-known case (Watson, 1930), a child who had played happily with a white rat was conditioned to fear the animal when a loud noise (UCS) was paired with sight of the rat (CS). The noise produced whimpering, falling forward, and other signs of discomfort. After several pairings of noise and rat, the child was distressed by the rat in the absence of the noise. Watson (1930) interpreted this experiment to mean that infants have only a few built-in emotional reactions, and that the bulk of adult fears are learned.

Later investigators have refined the techniques required to measure responses associated with emotion. During emotion a variety of changes occur simultaneously in the body, including acceleration of the heart rate, disturbance of breathing, and constriction of blood vessels. Usually it is not practical to record more than a few of these responses at one time, and many investigators limit their study to a single response. In measurement of emotion, a response of special interest is the *galvanic skin response.* It involves changes in the electrical resistance of the skin, and like other internal responses of the body, it may reflect the emotions of the individual. Since a person becomes somewhat emotional when he lies, the galvanic skin response often is measured as a part of lie detector tests.

INTERSTIMULUS INTERVAL

Classical conditioning is a result of pairing of the CS and UCS, but of what importance is the interstimulus interval? Simultaneous occurrence of the two stimuli is not a good way to produce conditioning. Optimum timing requires a short interval from onset of the CS to onset of the UCS. The optimal length of this interval depends upon the response being conditioned, the intensity of the CS, and characteristics of the organism. The relationship depicted in Figure 2 indicates a peak in the neighborhood of four tenths of a second. Figure 2 is based on human eyelid conditioning, in which the CS was a weak light and the UCS a puff of air to the cornea of the eye.

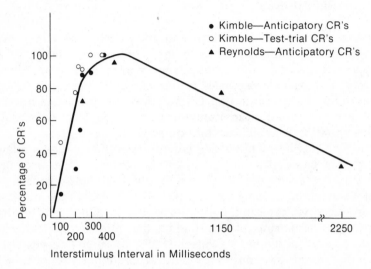

FIGURE 2   A smoothed curve showing the length of the interstimulus interval in relation to percentage of conditioned eyelid responses in human subjects.

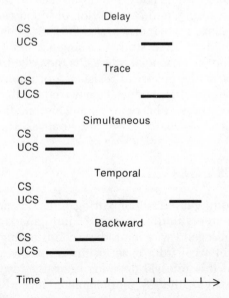

FIGURE 3   Several types of stimulus relationships in classical conditioning.

A number of other interstimulus arrangements can produce condition-ing, and the main variations are diagrammed in Figure 3. *Delay condition-ing* refers to the case in which the CS begins, usually a few seconds before the UCS, and continues until the UCS occurs. If the CS occurs briefly, always ending before the UCS starts, *trace conditioning* may develop. Pavlov assumed that some aftereffect or trace of the CS had to continue in order for conditioning to be effective under these circumstances. In *temporal conditioning* no explicit CS occurs, but instead the UCS is presented at regular intervals. The CS in this case is assumed to be some unknown event associated with the passage of time. As a final example, when the UCS precedes instead of follows the CS, conditioning does not seem to take place. The instances of *backward conditioning* that occasion-ally have been reported are generally considered to be the result of failure to control the experiment properly.

EXTINCTION

If the CS is presented in the absence of the UCS, the CR will occur less frequently. After many trials the CR may be eliminated, or *extinguished.* Even though the probability of a CR nears zero after a single session of extinction trials, the CR is not eliminated permanently. If the experi-mental animal is permitted to rest in its home quarters for a time after the extinction series, the CR will reappear spontaneously when the CS is again presented for test. The longer the rest period, the greater the degree of *spontaneous recovery* of the CR. The recovery occurs in the absence of further pairings of CS and UCS, although it is only temporary and not equal to the original degree of responding at the end of conditioning. With repeated extinction sessions, the amount of spontaneous recovery de-creases to zero.

The relationships between acquisition, extinction, and spontaneous recovery are illustrated in Figure 4 for the case of human eyelid condi-tioning (Hartman & Grant, 1960). Ignoring for the moment the differences between the four different conditions within each stage, note that the CR occurred with increasing frequency during acquisition. During extinction the rate decreased. When extinction was resumed after a rest interval, the CR's spontaneously recovered to some extent, but with further tests of the CS alone the CR's reached new lows in frequency of occurrence.

PARTIAL REINFORCEMENT

The UCS is known as a *reinforcing stimulus,* and trials on which the UCS is paired with the CS are called *reinforced* trials. At first thought it might seem that strength of the CR is a simple function of number of pairings or reinforcements. However, there are other factors to be considered, such as the effect of nonreinforced trials in which the CS is presented alone at

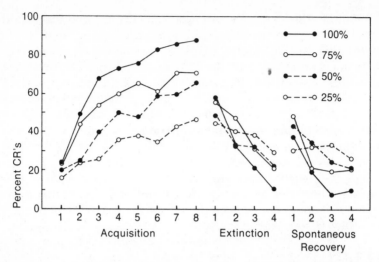

FIGURE 4   Percentages of conditioned responses during successive eighths of acquisition, extinction, and a second extinction session. The four conditions differed in percentage of reinforced trials during acquisition. Spontaneous recovery is present in the second extinction session.

random points during acquisition. The study graphed in Figure 4 involved four conditions with different schedules of reinforcement during acquisition. All groups of human subjects received forty reinforced trials. One group had all reinforced trials, the 100-percent condition. The other conditions had nonreinforced trials in addition, as in the 50-percent condition which had forty nonreinforced trials interspersed irregularly among the reinforced trials.

The *partial-reinforcement* conditions, in which nonreinforced trials were included, conditioned slowly, and the greater the number of nonreinforced trials the slower the learning. This seems plausible considering that these nonreinforced trials are extinction trials. However, a reversal occurred during extinction, for nonreinforced trials during acquisition resulted in more CR's during extinction. Thus subjects in the partial-reinforcement conditions were slower to extinguish in spite of the lower level of responding at the end of acquisition.

GENERALIZATION AND DISCRIMINATION

When an organism has been conditioned to respond to a particular CS, it will also tend to respond to other similar stimuli. For example, a dog conditioned to salivate to a tone of 256 cps will also salivate to a lesser degree to tones of 280 or 225 cps. This *stimulus generalization* of the CR is directly related to the similarity of the test stimulus to the original CS.

If the animal is to discriminate among stimuli, respond to one tone and not respond to another similar tone, specific procedures are used. *Discrimination* results from the use of nonreinforced trials with one stimulus while reinforced trials are given with the other stimulus. Thus, the response is conditioned to one stimulus and extinguished to the other. After many of these two kinds of trials, the animal will perform the CR on the presentation of the reinforced stimulus and refrain from responding to the nonreinforced stimulus. Discrimination training differs from the partial-reinforcement technique in that a different stimulus is present on the nonreinforced trials. In the partial-reinforcement procedures, the same CS occurs on all trials.

In the human adult, similarity often involves the meaning of words, rather than similarity of sensory qualities. Razran (1939) studied *semantic generalization* by conditioning adults to salivate to certain words. The subjects watched a screen while they ate food or chewed gum. Each word flashed on the screen fifteen times, including "style" and "urn." After two conditioning sessions, salivation to a variety of words was measured by weighing rolls of dental cotton which had been placed in the subjects' mouths. Salivation was greater to synonyms of the original words, such as "fashion" and "vase," than to homonyms such as "stile" and "earn." Razran concluded that subjects had been conditioned to the meaning of the words rather than to such sensory properties as sound and appearance. This generalization depended on past learning, the verbal learning of subjects prior to the experimental sessions.

HIGHER-ORDER CONDITIONING

The CS from an earlier conditioning experiment can be used as the basis for new conditioning. *Second-order conditioning* occurs when a new neutral stimulus is paired with the CS from previous conditioning, and the CR becomes conditioned to the new stimulus. Pavlov (1928) described a case in which salivation was conditioned to the ticking of a metronome. After conditioning was firmly established, a black square was paired with the metronome for a number of trials. Eventually the black square elicited salivation by itself, although less than that produced by the metronome. This salivation to the black square is a second-order CR.

The process might be continued for higher orders of conditioning. However, extinction of the previous CS occurs at the same time as the new conditioning, since the old CS is no longer paired with the UCS. For this reason higher-order conditioning tends to be relatively unstable, save in the conditioning of fear reactions.

INDIVIDUAL DIFFERENCES

One might expect differences in rate of conditioning to exist among individuals. This is the case, but the nature of the differences is not obvious. The rate of acquisition of a CR does not differ for persons of low intelligence as compared with individuals of average intelligence. On the other hand, personality tests are of some value in distinguishing between fast and slow conditioners. A paper-and-pencil test that was designed to measure anxiety, the Taylor Manifest Anxiety Scale, has been administered to groups of individuals, and conditioning observed for subjects measuring high in anxiety compared with those low on the scale (Taylor, 1951). As can be seen in Figure 5, those high in anxiety conditioned faster than those who were low in anxiety.

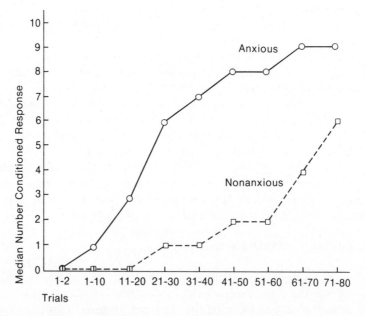

FIGURE 5 Learning curves for human eyelid conditioning showing differences for subjects scoring high and low on the Taylor Manifest Anxiety Scale.

INTERPRETATION

On a theoretical level, scientists have debated the extent to which classical conditioning can be the basis for learning. Some have considered the conditioned response the basic unit out of which most complex behavior can be compounded. Other theorists have seen in classical conditioning certain elementary principles which also can be applied to more complex behavior, although they do not view it as simply a compounding of CR's. Still others have viewed classical conditioning as deceptively simple, and not a fruitful source of insights for most complex behavior.

Many early theorists thought that conditioning involved direct substitution of one stimulus for another, as in Figure 6. One objection to this stimulus-response (S-R) interpretation of conditioning is that the CR is not always identical to the UCR. This is dramatically illustrated in the conditioning of heart rate, in which shock is used as the UCS. The UCR that occurs to the shock is a speeding up of the heart rate. The CR, however, is a slowing down of the heart (Notterman, Shoenfeld, & Bersh, 1952). Clearly the representation of classical conditioning shown in Figure 6 is not appropriate to conditioning of heart rate. Even in less dramatic instances, there may be subtle differences in the conditioned response, so that the CR must be described separately from the UCR.

FIGURE 6   Stimulus-response interpretation of classical conditioning. The dashed line indicates a newly formed relationship, while the solid line indicates a relationship established prior to the conditioning session.

An alternative formulation of what happens in classical conditioning has been called a stimulus-stimulus (S-S) interpretation as contrasted with the S-R interpretation of Figure 6. Instead of establishing a direct connection in the nervous system from sensory organ to the response mechanism, the relationship is between a representation of the CS and a representation of the UCS. Rather than the CR being an automatic reaction to the CS, a representation of the UCS is evoked which in turn leads to appropriate action which may or may not be identical to the UCR. In this way, *mediating events* intervene between the presentation of the CS and the occurrence of the CR.

It might be argued that the S-R interpretation applies to simple cases, whereas with verbal humans mediating events affect the response. Spence (1966) investigated extinction of eyelid conditioning in humans after an acquisition schedule involving only reinforced trials. In this case extinction usually is rapid compared with extinction among nonverbal animals. Extinction of the eyelid response after a continuous reinforcement schedule occurred in a trial or two, and Spence suggested that humans speed extinction by verbal inhibitory processes. When he embedded an eyelid-conditioning experiment with human subjects within the framework of another experiment which was the apparent interest of the experimenter, extinction occurred much more slowly than when typical eyelid conditioning was carried out. The verbal facilities of the subjects presumably were occupied with the diversionary experiment, leaving the conditioning and extinction to proceed in a simple form.

What is the importance of classical conditioning for understanding learning? From the practical point of view it is a technique for influencing emotional tendencies. It is of little value to debate whether conditioning principles should be used, since they are used from the brainwashing of prisoners to the advertising campaigns of business. The same principles are followed by teachers and parents in producing a socialized child. From another point of view, a knowledge of the techniques by which an individual's emotions have been influenced from an early age can help one understand emotional behavior in others. Knowledge of conditioning principles can also make us sensitive to the ways in which our own behavior is being influenced.

From a theoretical point of view, classical conditioning is a laboratory arrangement in which variables related to learning can be precisely measured, permitting experimenters to discover lawful relationships basic to learning. The concepts of conditioning, extinction, discrimination, and generalization offer a systematic way to interpret learning. To what extent conditioning concepts can account for more complex kinds of learning has been debated by theorists. In the next chapter conditioning concepts will be extended to a different class of experiments.

2

Instrumental Conditioning

A second type of conditioning is based on the principle that behavior is influenced by its consequences. Parents employ this principle when they reward or punish their children while animal trainers use it to develop repertoires of tricks in dogs, bears, monkeys, and creatures of many kinds. *Instrumental conditioning* entails making some consequence depend on performance of a response. When your dog raises its paw in your presence and you toss it a bit of food, it will perform this response with increasing frequency if reward continues to follow the lifting of the paw.

B. F. Skinner (1953) has systematically investigated the role of rewards in simplified laboratory settings for many years. One objective was to find some convenient unit of analysis and devise an automated apparatus to study it with maximum control of the variables involved. The response in early studies with rats was a bar press which could be recorded readily as well as rewarded automatically. Later Skinner studied the pecking of an illuminated disc, using pigeons as subjects. Hopefully, the principles obtained from these experiments could be extended to behavior in general. Furthermore, principles obtained from data on rats and pigeons might also apply to animals of a more complex nature, such as humans. Evidence that some generality of the principles exists has been obtained from similar experiments with human children, retardates, and patients in mental hospitals.

Skinner referred to the response in his apparatus as a free operant, free because the behavior could be performed at any rate, at any time. It was an operant in the sense of being a kind of operation on the environment, for example, pressing a bar. This learning was called *operant conditioning* by Skinner, although it is more generally included in the term *instrumental conditioning.* The latter term refers to a broader class of experimental situations in which an effect such as reward is made to depend on occurrence of some previous response, including instances in which the organism can respond only at times designated by the experimenter.

REINFORCEMENT IN INSTRUMENTAL CONDITIONING

Reinforcement is the fundamental concept in operant and instrumental conditioning; it refers to the reward or other consequence that is supplied after a specified response occurs. In contrast to classical conditioning, in which the experimenter can evoke the UCR by presentation of the UCS, one must wait for the desired response to occur, whereupon it is reinforced.

Shaping

When the response to be reinforced is slow in appearing, a technique called shaping can be used. Responses that resemble the desired response are reinforced, and the criterion for reinforcement is gradually shifted from the approximation toward the desired response. Suppose one wishes to train a white rat to push a marble across the floor of its cage. At first, the rat can be reinforced for being near the marble. Then, when it limits its movements to the vicinity of the marble, the reinforcement can be withheld until the rat actually touches the marble. When it touches the marble frequently, again the criterion can be changed to require something closer to the end result. By reinforcing *successive approximations,* the animal may be guided into performance of an otherwise unlikely behavior.

Chaining

Complicated sequences of behavior can be conditioned instrumentally by conditioning individual components and combining them into a chain of responses. Some act in the sequence is conditioned first, and then additional components are added one by one. If one wishes to teach a rat to pull a string in order to obtain marbles which can be used in a vending machine which dispenses food, a start is made by shaping the animal to push a marble as described earlier. As the rat becomes proficient at this, food is withheld unless the marble is pushed into a hole in the floor where it can trip the food-delivery mechanism. Then, a string in the ceiling is introduced, and string-pulling is reinforced with presentation of the marble. The rat will learn to make appropriate responses to the string, followed by the previously learned series of responses to the marble. This may take some time over a number of days, but animals usually are able to put together a chain of acts which end in a reinforcement. A similar analysis of complex behaviors into components can be accomplished in many other situations by starting with the final responses in the sequence and working backward to the beginning. The complexity of the behavior taught to the animal may be limited more by the patience and ingenuity of the trainer than by the intelligence of the animal.

Schedules of Reinforcement

The concept of partial reinforcement has already been introduced in the earlier discussion of classical conditioning. Investigation of a variety of partial reinforcement schedules were carried out by Skinner in his study of operant conditioning.

Work on scheduling of reinforcements started with a practical problem: Skinner was running short of food pellets one weekend, so he decided to ration them. He discovered that once an animal was responding the number of reinforcements required to maintain the behavior could be reduced, and the rat would continue to work even though minutes might elapse between reinforcements. The first response after a designated interval of time was reinforced, and then there would be no reinforcement for another interval. A *fixed-interval* schedule of this kind results in slow responding for a time after a reinforcement, but as the end of the interval approaches, there is a speeding up of the responding. In the terms of operant investigators, a schedule in which the reinforcement follows the first response after each interval of five minutes is called FI5.

Another schedule reinforces an organism for a set number of responses, say, one reinforcement for every three responses. Such an arrangement is called a *fixed-ratio* schedule, FR3 in this case. Its use speeds up the rate of responding markedly over the continuous reinforcement schedule in which a pellet is given for every response. In human terms, the animal is being paid for a certain amount of work, in contrast to the paycheck at regular intervals that is characteristic of a fixed-interval schedule.

Frequently schedules having unpredictable characteristics are useful. A *variable-interval* schedule is one in which the learner is reinforced after intervals of time that vary in an irregular way, as when the fisherman is rewarded at unexpected times. Such a schedule is designated by the average length of the intervals used. For instance, in an experiment in which intervals vary irregularly over a range of 5 to 120 seconds, the mean interval might be one minute (VI1).

A variable-interval schedule produces a steady rate of responding, making it possible to study changes due to experimental treatment. For example, suppose that one wanted to test a particular drug's influence on behavior. First, the animal is trained to respond at a steady rate with a variable-interval schedule, after which the drug is introduced. If the response rate changed after giving the drug, it may be inferred that the drug produced the effect.

In a *variable-ratio* schedule the reinforcements also are unpredictable, but in this case it is ratios of responses which change in an irregular fashion. An example is the slot machine which is programmed to reward the gambler after an unpredictable number of plays. A high rate of responding results from this schedule.

The schedules just described are only a few of the many schedules and combinations of schedules that are used in contemporary operant conditioning.

EXTINCTION

When an animal has been reinforced for responding, *extinction* is studied by stopping the reinforcement. Following removal of reinforcement, the learner's rate of responding decreases back to or lower than the original rate prior to conditioning.

Extinction furnishes a method of changing undesirable behavior. Parents should look for the reinforcement that maintains objectionable behavior in their child and try to eliminate the reinforcement. If the child demands service in loud unpleasant tones, the busy parent may have shaped the child by attending only when the child spoke in a disagreeable way. By withholding attention until an acceptable manner of speaking occurs, the obnoxious behavior may extinguish.

Extinction procedures do not always produce quick results. The characteristics of behavior during extinction are related to the schedule that was in effect during conditioning. Extinction after continuous reinforcement is relatively rapid, although there may be emotional flurries of rapid responding when behaviors such as biting the bar accompany the responses. The equivalent emotional behavior in the child might be kicking or crying.

The amount of responding in extinction is related to the number of reinforcements received during conditioning. The more reinforcements, the more responses will be likely to occur in extinction. However, other factors influence rate of responding. After a partial reinforcement schedule, extinction proceeds more slowly than after continuous reinforcement. For instance, after a variable-interval schedule there may be quite a long period of stable responding before responses get back to the unconditioned rate. Veteran fishermen may continue their bait-casting for a very long time even though no fish strikes.

Whatever the schedule, if responding has been extinguished and the learner is removed from the situation, *spontaneous recovery* usually occurs. When the animal is placed again in the experimental setting, responses occur at a rate above the unconditioned rate. Spontaneous recovery makes the attempt to extinguish human habits more difficult. The child's whining may recur from time to time even though the parents scrupulously refrain from reinforcing it.

CONDITIONED REINFORCERS

What kinds of stimuli are reinforcing? Food and water are easy to identify; they are *primary reinforcers*, required for the survival of the species. The effectiveness of primary reinforcers can be maximized by depriving the animal for a period of time.

Other kinds of events, having no biological function, may also serve as reinforcers. The neutral stimuli which accompany food or water may come to be reinforcing in themselves. A light which precedes feeding may become reinforcing. The click which is heard in a lever-pressing device when food is delivered can be reinforcing in the absence of food. New responses can be conditioned by the use of *conditioned* or *secondary reinforcers.* Sounds, sights, smells—any of these stimuli—can become reinforcers through learning.

One role that secondary reinforcers play lies in establishing chains of behavior. For instance, in the chain described earlier in which the rat pulled a string and deposited a marble in a tube, the marble can be considered a secondary reinforcer since it reinforced string-pulling and it had been linked to food. Other studies have shown that monkeys will work for poker chips when the chips can later be exchanged for food. In comparison, human beings work for money, a secondary reinforcer of great strength.

Discrimination and Generalization

Secondary reinforcers can have a signal function; they are cues for a predictable event which follows. When the function of a stimulus as a signal for what will follow is to be emphasized, the stimulus is called discriminative, and can be used to produce the behavior which has become appropriate to it. Discrimination is produced in operant and instrumental conditioning using basically the same procedures as in classical conditioning. The animal is reinforced for making the response in the presence of one stimulus but is not reinforced for emitting the response to other stimuli. Thus, stimuli can acquire the capacity to control operant or instrumental behavior, even though they could not prior to conditioning.

Discrimination can be demonstrated in the dog previously reinforced for lifting the paw. Reinforce him for lifting the paw when you say "Shake," and withhold reinforcement when the lifting occurs in response to anything else you say. The animal may eventually learn to hold out the paw only to this signal. Initially the animal may respond in the same way to many words that you speak, illustrating *generalization* in instrumental conditioning. Nevertheless, the animal will become more selective with continued discrimination training.

Various dimensions of similarity may be used in order to study generalization. In the case of sounds it could be pitch or intensity, while in the case of lights it could be brightness or position. However, learning of discriminations is limited by the sense organ involved; for example color-blind animals cannot learn to discriminate between colors.

PUNISHMENT

Aversive stimuli are used as unconditioned stimuli in many classical conditioning experiments, and it may seem that experimenters are punishing their subjects. However, punishment is not a pure case of classical conditioning, but rather is viewed as a subclass of instrumental conditioning. In spanking a child who has run into the street, an aversive stimulus is presented after the response in order to decrease the rate of responding. This is a case of instrumental conditioning, although there may also be classical conditioning of fear for the punisher.

The aversive stimulus in the study illustrated by Figure 7 was an annoying buzz (Azrin & Holz, 1966). The responses were moving either a knob or a pushbutton which were reinforced with cigarettes on a variable-interval schedule. The steepest cumulative curve in Figure 7 indicates a high rate of responding when no punishment was given. When a response produced a loud buzz as well as a cigarette, the rate of responding decreased, although there still was a substantial rate of responding. When there was an alternative response available which delivered cigarettes without punishment, punishment was highly effective, as the lowest, flattest curve indicates.

The use of punishment depends on a number of limiting factors. Punishment is not always socially desirable, since strong aversive stimulation may result in fear or anxiety becoming conditioned to various stimuli present at the time. Some individuals report strong negative

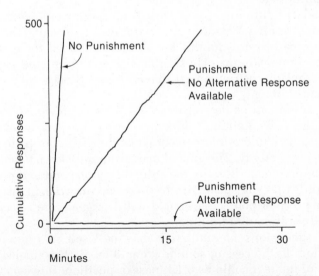

FIGURE 7   Cumulative response records of responses with a variable-interval schedule of reinforcement. The punishment was an annoying buzz. Note that in a cumulative curve the steeper the slope, the faster the response rate.

emotions aroused by persons who have punished them. Another reason for not using punishment is that it may be only temporarily effective. The effect of punishment usually wears off after the punishment is discontinued. The permanence of the effects of punishment depends on a number of factors, one being the severity of the aversive stimulation. If aversive stimulation is very intense, suppression of the response may continue indefinitely. Unfortunately, intensity of aversive stimulation also is related to maladaptive side effects. Under some circumstances animals have been known to starve rather than to perform a response that was punished (Solomon, 1964). Availability of another response to take the place of the punished response must also be considered with the use of punishment. If an alternate response is rewarded in the situation in which the original response was punished, an animal is less likely to go back to the punished response.

AVOIDANCE AND ESCAPE TRAINING

Under some circumstances a response can be learned which prevents an aversive stimulus from occurring. If some stimulus regularly precedes the aversive stimulus stimulation, humans and animals can learn to anticipate it and do something to avoid it. If a tone sounds five seconds before electric current activates the floor of a cage, an animal may learn to avoid the shock by hurdling a barrier or performing some other response that is effective in the situation. Humans watch the skies and take precautionary measures when a storm seems imminent, thus avoiding unfortunate consequences.

Avoidance training should be distinguished from *escape training.* In the latter the aversive stimuli occur and then are terminated by a response. In *avoidance training* the aversive stimuli do not occur if the designated response is performed. In situations where aversive stimulation can be neither avoided nor escaped, *conditioned helplessness* may result. When no way out can be discovered, animals may stop making exploratory responses. If the possibility for escape or avoidance is offered later, the animal may not learn the adaptive response (Seligman, Maier, & Solomon, 1969).

We mentioned earlier that experimenters assume the laws of learning apply to responses generally, not just to the particular response which is convenient to study in the laboratory. It should now be acknowledged that not all responses are equally easy to condition, and that differences in difficulty of training are especially great in the case of avoidance training. It is not possible to train all rats to avoid a shock by pressing a lever, even though lever-pressing is not difficult to train by using food or water as a reinforcer. On the other hand it is easy to train a rat to jump out of a box in which it has been shocked, in some cases after a single training trial. One plausible explanation of wide differences in difficulty of training an avoidance response is that a given species of animal has specific defensive reactions to novel or sudden stimuli, and that such an innate response is easy to train as an avoidance response (Bolles, 1970). Other responses may be difficult or impossible to condition.

APPLICATIONS OF CONDITIONING PRINCIPLES

Interactions of Classical and Instrumental Conditioning

.In the normal course of life outside the laboratory, instances of classical and instrumental conditioning are closely intertwined. Even in the laboratory it is difficult to isolate pure cases of one or the other. In classical conditioning experiments the animal may make a response which reduces the effect of the unconditioned stimulus so that instrumental avoidance conditioning occurs. For instance, in eyelid conditioning an anticipatory blink may reduce the effectiveness of the air puff as an aversive stimulus. Similarly, in an experiment intended to study instrumental conditioning there inevitably is some pairing of stimuli which may produce classical conditioning.

One experimental arrangement in which the two varieties of conditioning are combined involves *conditioned suppression* of operant behavior (Estes & Skinner, 1941). An animal is reinforced with water or food for bar-pressing until it is responding at a stable rate. Then, a tone is sounded for a few minutes followed by an electric shock. After a number of pairings of the tone and shock, bar-pressing declines during the period that the tone is on.

The pairings of tone and shock are in the tradition of classical conditioning. The tone eventually elicits the emotional reaction that originally was evoked by the shock. This classically conditioned response disrupts or suppresses the bar-pressing, which was conditioned instrumentally. The interaction of two kinds of conditioning in this experimental arrangement serves as a demonstration of *conditioned anxiety.* Persons who become anxious tend to neglect other kinds of activity, and the conditioned emotional response shows the negative effect of emotion on adaptive behavior.

Instrumental Conditioning of Autonomic Responses

Traditionally it has been said that classical conditioning applies to involuntary responses mediated by the autonomic nervous system, while instrumental conditioning applies to voluntary responses activated by the skeletal nervous system. Recent experiments have raised questions concerning this generalization.

One point of interest has been well known for many years. It is possible to exercise at least some voluntary control over many presumably involuntary activities of the body (Katkin & Murray, 1968). Reports of instrumental conditioning of heart rate, galvanic skin response, and constriction of blood vessels indicate that organisms can exercise voluntary control over autonomic responses.

The mechanism for this conditioning is not entirely clear, but many possibilities for mediating events exist. For one thing, various autonomic responses are unconditioned responses to skeletal and respiratory movements. Deep breathing will produce changes in the galvanic skin response, so that one can change this autonomic response by breathing which is under voluntary control. Changes in the blood vessels follow from relaxing the skeletal muscles as well as altering depth of breathing.

In addition to autonomic control by means of voluntary muscle movements, one may expose oneself to emotional stimuli such as pictures and thereby excite the autonomic responses. Or one may produce internal images and by means of this central mediation produce changes in the autonomic responses.

None of these mediated ways of autonomic control satisfies criteria that psychologists require of direct instrumental conditioning. Instrumental conditioning of autonomic responses in animals that have been paralyzed by curare has been reported, which suggests direct instrumental conditioning of internal nonvoluntary responses is possible (Miller, 1969).

Practical interest centers on the fact that whether instrumental conditioning is direct or mediated, the effect of learning on functions of the viscera is significant. Psychosomatic illness may result from rewarding bodily distress, so it seems likely that some individuals learn to be sick because they are reinforced for it. The remedy is to stop reinforcing illness, a cure which may require educating parents and other agents of reinforcement.

Modification of Problem Behavior

Conditioning techniques are helpful in the treatment of some behavior problems. Consider the problem posed by children who do not have normal social interaction with others (Hingten & Trost, 1966); they say little and have little physical contact with other children. Training consisted in letting them press a lever to obtain coins which then could be used in a machine that dispensed food. After this preparation, the children were given vocal training in which they were rewarded for making sounds. Shaping was required, and at first any sound from a cough to a giggle was reinforced by a coin. When the frequency of these responses increased, reinforcement was given only for syllables. In addition to this vocal training given to individuals, children also were paired off and reinforced for interacting with each other. Again, shaping was required, but eventually there was a substantial increase in social interaction.

Lest it be thought that money and food are the only practical reinforcers with children, consider a case in which attention paid by adults was used as a reinforcer (Harris, Wolf, & Baer, 1964). A three-year-old girl spent most of her time in nursery school either crawling or crouching with her face hidden. A period of observation suggested that this behavior attracted the attention of her teachers, whereas standing and walking attracted no attention. A reversal in the arrangement had teachers ignore the child when she was crawling or crouching; only when she stood or walked or ran would the teachers respond to her. Within a week of beginning the new schedule, the child was walking in a normal fashion.

Some ingenious ways of programming punishment also have been reported. In one case thumb-sucking was punished by turning off a movie projector which was showing the child animated cartoons (Baer, 1962). Unfortunately, the punishment was effective only during periods immediately following its use. As in all cases of treatment using reinforcers and punishers, one problem is to get the effect to generalize to situations outside the treatment setting. In some instances parents and teachers can be persuaded to adopt criteria for reinforcement which will support the efforts of the clinic or laboratory. On occasion patients may learn to discriminate between the treatment room and other settings, so they revert to their usual ways outside the treatment setting. In some cases at least, desirable social behavior may be encouraged outside the treatment room, and if it then is reinforced naturally by the child's contacts, it may continue. If a child can be made to start to talk and play normally, he will be reinforced for it, and the behavior will be maintained by normal social interaction.

Operant techniques have been applied to adults hospitalized with behavior disorders by enlisting the cooperation of nurses and attendants in the development of *token economies* (Carlson, Hersen, & Eisler, 1972). Tokens were given to patients for behaviors such as performance of tasks, promptness at meals, and appropriate verbal behavior. The tokens were used to obtain special privileges including leave from the ward, attendance at recreational affairs, and purchase of trinkets and consumables. Patients became more manageable in this situation, and the frequency of socially approved behaviors increased.

Whether there is substantial transfer of improvement in behavior to the outside world is another question. Different reinforcement contingencies may operate in the individual's home environment, so the new behavior may extinguish. Furthermore, all of the patient's problems in the hospital setting may not be solved by such procedures. Nevertheless, token economies emphasize the influence that society has on our behavior through the administration of reinforcement.

Aversion Therapy

In addition to these applications of instrumental conditioning, techniques which are a combination of classical and instrumental procedures may be used. In the first stage aversive properties are conditioned to stimuli connected with some undesirable activity. For instance, the taste and smells associated with alcohol may be paired with drugs which produce nausea. In the second stage, the individual is expected to refrain from drinking alcohol to avoid the negative emotional reaction now produced by drinking alcohol. The first stage is classical conditioning, while the second involves instrumental avoidance conditioning.

Of course, when the drugs are stopped, the conditions for extinction are present, and the individual who is motivated to drink may do so in spite of temporary nausea. With each additional drink the conditioned nausea extinguishes further, making the method successful only when other factors support the treatment (Rachman & Teasdale, 1969). In the treatment of alcoholism, as in other problems treated by aversion therapy, the degree of success is limited by many factors in the individual case.

The application of instrumental conditioning principles to life outside the laboratory requires that we recognize the complexities involved. Reinforcement frequently is supplied by human beings rather than by machines, and other persons also provide many of the cues to be discriminated. Thus, reinforcement must be considered in the context of social interaction. Since the humans with whom we interact have long and complex learning histories which have accentuated individual differences among them, their behavior is less predictable than that of simpler organisms in a laboratory setting.

3

The Concept of Reinforcement

Instrumental conditioning studies have demonstrated clearly that reinforcement is an effective technique for altering behavior. Reinforcement can be defined empirically without any significant theoretical connotations, for instance in the manner of Skinner (1953). We observe the effect of an event on the frequency of occurrence of some previous response, and if the frequency changes the event is reinforcing. Again following Skinner, such events can be classified into two categories. Positive reinforcers are those which increase the performance of a response by their presentation, for instance, food and water. Negative reinforcers produce an increase in responding when they are removed following a response, for example, electric shock or loud noise. Punishment then is the presentation of a negative reinforcer or the removal of a positive reinforcer.

Like Skinner, one could stop with this simple classification of events and refuse to speculate on the reasons that reinforcement has such effects. Other experimenters have raised questions about the basis of reinforcement, and have conducted a variety of experiments to find the answers to these questions. We will make a brief survey of possible answers to two main questions about reinforcement: What is the common basis for the reinforcing effect, and is reinforcement necessary for learning to occur?

THE BASIC ELEMENT IN REINFORCEMENT

Drive Reduction

A number of theoretical attempts have been made to find a defining characteristic of reinforcement which would eliminate the necessity for trial and error in classifying reinforcers. One possible basis for reinforcement is the reduction of a physiological need (Hull, 1943). Food and water are reinforcing because they reduce the needs of hunger and thirst. If an event reduces a need, then it can be considered reinforcing without trying it out.

A need-reduction theory becomes somewhat more plausible if it is modified into a drive-reduction theory. Drive is a behavioral variable related to needs, and it may be more useful to speak of drive-reduction because not all physiological needs have the typical energizing effect on behavior that defines drives. For example, a lack of oxygen is a need, but it doesn't result in a drive. Neal Miller (1963) made drive even more specific by defining drives as strong stimuli, and suggested that drive-stimulus reduction is the common factor in all kinds of reinforcement. Reinforcement by escape from aversive stimulation is then not basically different from presentation of food and water, since in both cases the effect can be attributed to diminution of the strength of stimuli. In the one case the stimuli accompany hunger, and in the other they are produced by electric shock.

Onset of Stimulation

While it may be plausible that substances that reduce drives are reinforcing, other kinds of events also are reinforcing even though they do not involve drive reduction. Rats were conditioned to press a lever by reinforcing them with saccharin, a sweet-tasting substance without nutritive value (Sheffield & Roby, 1950). The saccharin was dissolved in water, and rate of lever-pressing was related to the degree of concentration of saccharin (Pfaffman, 1964). As the concentration of saccharin increased, the rate of lever-pressing also increased, up to a point. A very high concentration of saccharin did not produce an optimal rate, indicating that the water can get too sweet for a rat's taste. When the portion of the thalamic area which is active in taste perception has been made inactive, the rate of lever-pressing is lower, and there is no longer any relationship between amount of saccharin and rate of responding.

The effect of this nonnutritive reinforcer is not readily explained by reduction of anything, rather the reinforcement involves an increase in stimulation. At the least it is evidence against drive reduction as an adequate basis for reinforcement, and it offers for consideration onset of stimulation as the fundamental basis of reinforcement.

Another type of reinforcement that occurs with the onset of stimulation involves electrical activation of tiny electrodes inserted deep into the brain. Rats were tested in a device in which the pressing of a lever resulted in a pulse of electricity delivered to a specific point of electrode implantation. Certain places were found, many in the septal area, which when stimulated electrically resulted in reinforcement (Olds & Milner, 1954). When a lever turned on the electricity briefly, the rat pressed the lever at a rapid rate. There are other points, in the diencephalon, for which electrical stimulation is aversive, and rats will turn a wheel to stop the stimulation (Miller, 1957). There also are points in the hypothalamus which when stimulated cause a rat to press a bar to turn on the current, and then when the stimulation continues, rotate a wheel to turn it off.

Thus, both offset of stimulation as well as onset of stimulation are reinforcing depending on the location of the stimulation and other variables. Brain-stimulation studies provide evidence against a drive-reduction theory of reinforcement, but they do not offer conclusive evidence for an explanation in terms of onset of stimulation.

Activity Rate

Premack (1965) has suggested that the basic aspect of reinforcement lies in activity which occurs at a higher rate than the class of behavior being reinforced. He begins with an analysis of the natural rate of occurrence of various activities such as eating, drinking, running, and bar-pressing. These rates differ depending on the specific activity. An activity with a low rate can be reinforced by the opportunity to perform some activity with a higher rate. For instance, bar-pressing has a low base rate, so it can be reinforced by eating, which has a higher base rate.

The rate of doing any of these things is affected by such variables as how long the animal has been deprived of food, or how hard the lever is to press. The rankings can be changed by various experimental manipulations; under some circumstances, for instance, drinking can be reinforced by the opportunity to run, instead of the usual reverse relationship.

One way of looking at findings of this kind is to view rate of performance as a measure of the animal's preference for a given activity. Any less preferred activity can be made to occur more frequently if it is the means to another more preferred activity. This enlarges the scope of possible reinforcers, and drive-reduction is not essential.

IS REINFORCEMENT NECESSARY FOR LEARNING?

The results of the investigations of nonnutritive reinforcers, brain stimulation, and relative rates of activity suggest that reinforcement is not adequately explained in terms of any simple characteristic. The search for a basic ingredient has not produced a generally acceptable explanation of reinforcement. A broader question is whether reinforcement, however defined, is necessary for learning. Reinforcement theorists, such as Hull (1943), have made reinforcement a necessary prerequisite to learning. Granted that reinforcers of various kinds increase the frequency with which some response (or chain of responses) occurs, can there be learning without reinforcement?

Latent Learning and Extinction

Studies of latent learning are one attempt to answer this question. In these studies, animals have been permitted to explore mazes without finding reinforcement on early trials, and then on later trials reinforcement has been introduced at the end of the maze. These animals did almost as well as animals who were reinforced from the beginning in the maze. Apparently animals not fed in the maze learn something in spite of the lack of reinforcement; the learning is hidden or latent until the animals are motivated. Reinforcing events have a motivating effect on performance, but the absence of the reinforcer does not preclude learning.

Latent-extinction studies are a complement to latent-learning studies. Latent extinction follows an original learning task, when there is an opportunity to experience the changed reinforcement contingency without performing the response that was learned. For instance, after learning to run to a goal box where food was found, a rat is placed in the empty goal box without making a run. When the animal is later given conventional extinction trials in which running leads to an empty goal box, the previous look at the empty goal box speeds extinction.

Another approach is to partially extinguish responses during a drugged state in which responses cannot be performed. Black (1958) trained dogs to press a panel when they heard a tone, and by so doing they avoided shock. Then the dogs were given curare, paralyzing their skeletal muscles so that they had to have artificial respiration in order to breathe. The signal for shock (tone) was presented a number of times with no shock following, but due to the curare the animals could not respond. When the dogs were later extinguished after recovering from the drugs, they did so much more rapidly than animals who did not experience trials under curare.

Other studies with curare have shown that dogs can learn new responses as well as extinguish old responses without performing the responses in question. Actions of muscles and glands may support and aid learning, but learning can occur in the absence of peripheral responding. In the case of eating or drinking or running, it is not the activity itself that is essential for learning.

Auto-shaping

Additional research which raises questions about the role of reinforcement is *auto-shaping*. In auto-shaping a response is acquired even though it doesn't affect delivery of reinforcement; in fact, the response can be maintained even though it prevents reinforcement (Williams & Williams, 1969). The basic procedure involves a pigeon in an operant-conditioning device in which grain is used as a reinforcer. Several seconds before the food mechanism delivers the grain a disc lights up. After several pairings of the light and the food, most pigeons begin to peck the disc, even though the food is delivered regardless of whether or not the disc is pecked. Since the response develops without the need for shaping of successive approximations by the experimenter, it is called auto-shaping. The pigeon is shaping its own behavior, so to speak.

Once disc-pecking occurs, it is followed by food delivery; therefore, its maintenance might be thought to depend on instrumental reinforcement even though its first occurrence did not. But, consider a case in which pecking the disc turns off the light and prevents food delivery. The peck is no longer simply irrelevant, it is maladaptive since it prevents reinforcement. In spite of this, pigeons peck the disc at a substantial rate day after day, often enough to keep the amount of food obtained at a low level. Some strong factor maintains the behavior even though it works counter to reinforcement. It might involve some innate tendency specific to pigeons, but in any event it is a reminder that reinforcement is only one of a number of factors influencing behavior. Changes in behavior can occur, not only in the absence of reinforcement, but in opposition to it.

INCENTIVE MOTIVATION

In some situations, the larger the reward, the faster an animal runs. Is this an effect on learning, so that the larger reward builds a stronger habit? Or does amount of reward have only a temporary effect on performance?

Latent-learning studies have shown that learning can occur and not be reflected in performance until appropriate motivation is supplied. Performance requires both learning and motivation, but what determines the motivation of an organism? One factor is degree of deprivation, keeping an animal from eating or drinking or satisfying some other need.

A second component of motivation is incentive. Imagine two groups of animals that have learned to run from start box to goal box in a straight runway. Running time is measured, and the animals given the large reward run faster than those given the small reward. Now, both groups are switched to an amount of reward midway between the two extremes. If the difference in reward produces differences in strength of the running habit, the animals originally given the large reward still should be faster. But this does not turn out to be the case, instead the difference in speed disappears. Amount of reward influences momentary performance rather than learning, and hence it may be classified with degree of deprivation as another performance factor. It is referred to as *incentive motivation* to distinguish it from the motivation arising from deprivation. Incentive motivation arises from learning experiences in which the learner comes to anticipate the reinforcer.

An interpretation of reinforcement that suggests the animal anticipates reward is different from one that holds the action of reinforcement is an automatic strengthening of the previous habit. Anticipation and incentive motivation have been explained by Hull (1952) as complex learning arising from the basic process of reinforcement. When an organism is exposed repeatedly to some serial situation like a maze, a fractional part of the goal activity occurs implicitly in response to stimuli at the beginning of the sequence.

Anticipatory responses were Hull's term for symbolic behavior in animals. The rat's anticipation in the start box constituted a primitive kind of thinking, the fractional responses representing the whole activity from which they were derived. Some representation of the reinforcer becomes associated with the situation leading up to it, as when we think of food in the kitchen while walking up to the front door. This is incentive motivation, and it is considered by many to be a classically conditioned component of instrumental conditioning.

INFORMATION

From another point of view, reinforcement provides information. Information about the consequences of alternative responses can later be used as the basis of performance. From this same point of view, secondary reinforcers provide information about primary reinforcers. If a second redundant stimulus is added after an initial stimulus, it does not acquire the same degree of reinforcing capability as the first stimulus (Egger & Miller, 1962).

Other studies dealing with magnitude of reward suggest that monkeys remember relative amounts of reward associated with individual stimuli (Meyer, LoPopolo, & Singh, 1966). Rather than reinforcement automatically producing a habit, information about reward is stored. Similar experiments with humans permit questioning the subjects about their memory for characteristics of reward (Estes, 1966). The amount can be recalled with a fair degree of accuracy, indicating a storage of information about reward.

AWARENESS

Is the human being aware of what is happening when reinforcement occurs? From what has been said about information, the reader might conclude that humans must be aware of the reinforcement contingency, but this is not necessarily the case. When one questions subjects who have been reinforced for verbal responses, the only ones who are unable to report the basis for reinforcement are likely to be those who were not conditioned successfully (Spielberger & DeNike, 1966). On the other hand, in some studies involving nonverbal responses, subjects seem unaware of being conditioned.

Consider an experiment in which the subjects were told that the experimenters were interested in the effects of noise superimposed on music (Hefferline, Keenan, & Harford, 1959). Sets of electrodes were attached to various parts of the body, and the subjects were told to listen to the music and do nothing else. From time to time as the music was heard, an aversive loud hum would occur. The hum could be eliminated if the subject made a small, normally invisible movement in the left thumb. Movements of the muscles in the left thumb were measured electrically and monitored on a meter by the experimenter. In spite of the obscurity of the response, it was conditioned. The subjects were unaware of what was happening to them and were surprised to learn later that they themselves had controlled the hum. Control subjects were unable to perform the response deliberately in small enough magnitude to satisfy the criterion for reinforcement.

Conditioning may occur, then, even though subjects are not able to report what has happened. However, when the response is obvious, the subject usually can report the reinforcement contingency.

In summary, the empirical principle of reinforcement is very useful in understanding the modification of behavior. If one supplies reinforcers following some behavior, that behavior will increase in frequency. The search for a common denominator underlying events that are reinforcing has not resulted in a generally accepted independent criterion of reinforcement. Classifications in terms of drive-reduction, onset of stimulation, or relative rate of activity are of limited usefulness.

The distinction between learning and performance clarifies some problems related to the interpretation of reinforcement. Performance is dependent on both learning and motivation. Reinforcement affects performance through incentive motivation, since reinforcers can also be called incentives that motivate performance. Latent-learning studies indicate that learning can occur in the absence of clearly definable reinforcement and can be demonstrated later when appropriate motivating conditions are introduced. Learning includes the acquisition of information about various relationships in the environment, including location and amount of reward. In this way incentives acquire their motivating properties through learning.

4

Learning to Discriminate

Learning to discriminate one stimulus from similar stimuli is so important in our everyday life that psychologists have done a great deal of research to try to understand the process. Many questions have arisen, such as "Is the learning of an individual discrimination a gradual, continuous process, or does it involve sudden insight?"

A CONTINUITY INTERPRETATION

Summation of Excitation and Inhibition

One theory of discrimination learning views it as a summing up of the positive effects of conditioning trials together with the negative effects of extinction trials (Spence, 1937). The response to a cue of the experimenter's choice is consistently reinforced trial after trial, until the cue gradually acquires the power to evoke the response. This positive cue has excitatory strength in respect to the stimulus-response relationship. Through generalization other similar stimuli have some lesser positive strength in relation to the response. On the other hand, the stimulus which is presented with the response on extinction trials gradually acquires a negative value. Its appearance tends to inhibit the response, and stimuli similar to it also inhibit the response, though in lesser degree. The likelihood of any stimulus on this dimension of similarity evoking the response depends on the algebraic sum of the positive value and the negative value of that stimulus.

In everyday life, stimuli differ from one another in many characteristics; however, for the sake of simplicity stimuli are chosen for laboratory experiments in discrimination learning so that they vary on only one dimension. After discrimination training, stimuli on various points along the dimension can be tested for their evocative power. A *generalization gradient,* or a graded series of measures of response strength, can be graphed to show how stimulus similarity is related to the stimulus-response relationship that has been acquired.

In Figure 8 hypothetical generalization gradients have been plotted separately for excitatory and inhibitory components. They are based on discrimination training in which two stimulus objects alike in all respects save area were used (Spence, 1937). Responses to a stimulus which was 256 centimeters square were reinforced, while responses to a stimulus 160 centimeters square went unreinforced. Generalization gradients developed around each stimulus value. The height of a point on the gradient indicates the strength of the response to a stimulus at that value. The solid curve represents a positive gradient with peak strength at the value that was reinforced, while the dashed curve represents a negative gradient with its peak at the stimulus value that was not reinforced. These excitatory and inhibitory gradients combine algebraically at each size along the stimulus dimension, and generalization tests would be expected to produce an empirical generalization gradient reflecting this summation of positive and negative components.

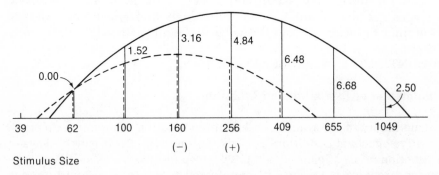

FIGURE 8   Representation of a hypothetical positive gradient after reinforcement on the stimulus value 256, and a negative gradient after nonreinforcement of the stimulus value 160.

Peak Shift

The summation theory predicts that the greatest response strength should occur not to the originally rewarded stimulus value, but at a point on the dimension farther away from the nonreinforced stimulus value. This predicted *peak shift* is found in empirical generalization gradients such as the one graphed on the right of Figure 9. In contrast, the gradient on the left peaks at the value that was reinforced. This latter gradient was obtained following training without a cue that was not reinforced, i.e., there was no discrimination training.

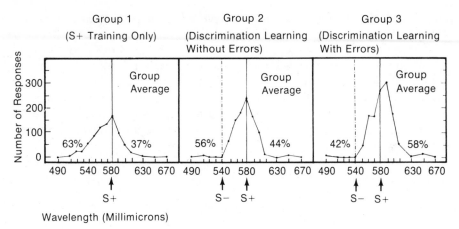

FIGURE 9 Empirical generalization gradients showing a peak shift after standard discrimination training and absence of a shift after errorless training.

The graph in the center of Figure 9 shows no peak shift even though it is based on data obtained after discrimination training. Special gradual training procedures were used with pigeons, so that they learned to discriminate without making the usual errors that accompany discrimination training. This was accomplished by introducing the negative stimulus very briefly at a low intensity, and then gradually increasing its brightness and duration as training continued. The discovery that discriminations can be learned virtually without error in some situations is intriguing in itself, and the absence of the peak shift adds to the interest (Terrace, 1964).

Transposition

A problem which can be related to peak shift concerns *transposition.* After two stimuli on some dimension have been successfully used in discrimination training, a new combination of stimuli from the same dimension is presented. Suppose that the brighter of two shades of paper has been reinforced, and now that shade is tested along with an even brighter shade. Will the animal respond to the absolute brightness value that was previously reinforced, or will it choose the brighter of the two presented? In many experiments, animals from chickens to humans choose the brighter of the two, suggesting that they have learned to respond to a relationship rather than to an absolute value of the stimulus.

A summation theory can explain some instances of transposition as a peak shift in the gradient of generalization. The excitatory strength is assumed to be greater at some value other than the one reinforced. The summation theory also would predict a reversal in the relative strength of two cues, if the cues were taken from a more remote part of the dimension; this has been found in some experiments.

Transposition can be explained in other ways, not involving the summation of generalization gradients. Monkeys and humans respond to relationships under circumstances when a summation theory does not seem applicable. It should be noted that Spence intended his theory for use with simple animals, and made no attempt to explain human adult behavior. Even with lower animals alternative explanations of transposition are possible.

A NONCONTINUITY INTERPRETATION

Hypothesis Testing

In contrast to the continuity view of discrimination learning, noncontinuity theorists consider such learning to be achieved suddenly. At some point in the training, progress occurs very rapidly, frequently after a period of little improvement. Discrimination learning is viewed as a problem-solving situation in which organisms try out one solution after another until they hit upon the one that works.

Karl Lashley (1942) suggested that position responses, for example, going left each time, were not chance behaviors but represented an attempt to solve a problem. Similarly, responding to an irrelevant cue—brightness as opposed to shape—was another attempted solution. These attempts were the result of unknown internal factors related to perception and attention. The animal did not respond to all of the components of the stimulating situation equally but reacted initially to some and later to others.

Systematic error tendencies are called "hypotheses," and they supposedly are controlled by internal factors including past experience. Because the organism is testing hypotheses, learning is not continuous from beginning to end of the training. While the animal is attending to the wrong cue, he is not learning in relation to the right cue. Learning of the correct response begins when the right hypothesis is tested, after which learning may proceed rapidly.

Reversal of Cues

One way to distinguish experimentally between these two views of discrimination learning is to change the reinforcement assignment before the animal has stopped making errors. If the animal was rewarded for approaching a square in the beginning of the experiment, he might be rewarded for approaching a circle. The continuity view would predict that learning would be slowed by such a change, while a noncontinuity view would predict no slowing if the change took place before the animal hit upon the right hypothesis.

Experimental tests with rats have produced mixed results, but the continuity position is generally supported. It takes longer to reach the criterion when the reinforcement contingency is changed at some point. On the other hand, experiments with sophisticated humans do not support a continuity interpretation of discrimination learning. In a typical experiment with geometrical figures as stimuli, subjects who were shifted to a new reinforcement contingency after five trials were no slower in reaching the criterion than subjects for whom the contingency was not shifted (Bower & Trabasso, 1964).

Overtraining

Cues can be reversed after the criterion of learning has been reached, and in this case, according to a continuity interpretation, the longer an animal is trained on one stimulus-response-reinforcement combination, the stronger that habit should become. The more trials that an animal is given after reaching the criterion, the harder it should be to reverse the discrimination. When discrimination reversals are tested after various degrees of overtraining, it frequently is found that it is easier to reverse after much overtraining than after little overtraining (Sperling, 1965). Thus, the continuity view is not supported by this finding.

LEARNING TO LEARN

In the studies just described that dealt with lower animals, a continuity interpretation is supported for animals naive to the experimental task. On the other hand, a noncontinuity interpretation generally is appropriate for animals with considerable experience in the task. Is it possible that both views are correct, but that they apply to different stages of learning?

A view of insightful learning developing only after extensive training on various tasks has strong support in the work of Harlow (1949). He observed monkeys as they learned hundreds of simple discriminations of a similar kind. He discovered that when organisms learn many tasks, they don't just accumulate a lot of individual habits, but they *learn how to learn.*

Object Discrimination

Learning to learn has been studied extensively with the Wisconsin General Test Apparatus shown in Figure 10. On a given problem the monkey is confronted with a choice between two objects, for instance, a cube versus a round cylinder. If the monkey lifts the appropriate object, it finds a grape underneath it. On succeeding trials, the position of the correct object is changed in an irregular fashion. Since it cannot be successful consistently on the basis of position, the animal learns to respond to a particular object, although it is a slow process in a naive animal.

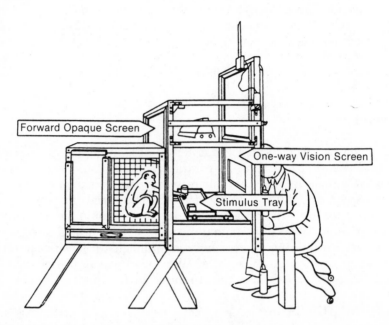

FIGURE 10   The Wisconsin General Test Apparatus.

So far we have described nothing more than simple discrimination learning, but the distinguishing feature emerges after further training. In a typical program each monkey may learn 300 or 400 object discriminations, with each new problem having a different pair of objects. In the experiment summarized in Figure 11, each monkey learned 344 different problems. For the first 32 problems each of the eight monkeys was given fifty trials per problem, while for the next 200 problems each monkey had six trials on a problem. Finally, on the last 112 problems an average of nine trials was given per problem.

Was there any difference in method of solution, as the monkeys became more and more experienced? Differences can be inferred from the shape of the learning curves. The earliest curve (1–8) is an S-shaped curve that frequently is found with naive animals, and is generally thought to provide evidence for trial-and-error learning. Note the curve for Problems 25–32, when there was a considerable amount of learning from the first trial on a new problem, remembering that on the first trial the monkey is likely to be right by chance 50 percent of the time.

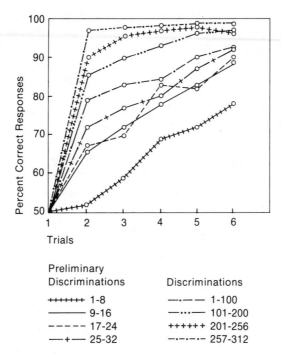

FIGURE 11   Discrimination learning curves for successive blocks of problems.

In the upper curve of Figure 11, averaged over the last problems, the monkeys were almost 100 percent accurate on the second trial of a new problem. They learned the correct choice on the first trial, and they learned it whether their response was right or wrong. Since a wrong choice was not reinforced, this learning is more complex than simple instrumental conditioning. The monkeys displayed insightful, intelligent behavior after their many experiences. They had learned how to learn quickly.

What was learned in these experiments? For one thing, the monkeys learned not to respond to irrelevant features of the situation. Various error tendencies had to be unlearned; for example, the monkeys had to learn not to respond to position, since the side which was correct was randomly determined. They had to learn not to continue with an initially preferred stimulus, when responding to this stimulus was not reinforced. They were learning to respond to selected cues and to ignore the others.

Discrimination Reversals

More complex kinds of learning have been investigated by similar techniques. Having learned object discriminations in the manner just described, monkeys can learn *discrimination reversals.* At some point after a number of trials on a problem, the rewarded object is no longer rewarded. This point is reached after some unpredictable number of trials; it could be seven or nine or eleven. A learning-to-learn curve for eight monkeys given 112 reversal problems is shown in Figure 12. It shows percent of correct choices on the second trial after reversal, which is the first choice after the formerly correct response had gone un-rewarded. At first when problems of this kind were introduced, respond-ing was near chance level just after the reversal. After a number of similar problems, choices on this trial reached nearly 100 percent correct. In spite of the many rewards of the original task which presumably should make that habit strong, the monkeys reversed after a single unrewarded choice. In conditioning terminology, this would be one-trial extinction. From another point of view it is insightful behavior at the end of a long series of training problems.

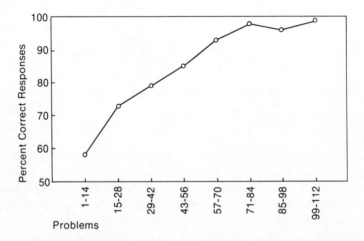

FIGURE 12   Discrimination-reversal learning-set curve based on Trial 2 responses.

Dimensional Shifts

Learning to learn has been studied with young children, and the results parallel those found with monkeys. Naive children learn slowly, whereas after many problems of a given type they learn to learn. However, older children and adults have a long history of learning on many varieties of tasks, so that it is not easy to find a simple task on which they will be sufficiently naive to exhibit gradual improvement.

Changes in the reinforcement contingency after learning has been achieved throw some light on discrimination learning in children at various ages. Comparison of a discrimination reversal with a shift to a new dimension yields interesting conclusions (Kendler & Kendler, 1962). Consider a task in which an initial discrimination is learned on the basis of size, so that subjects make a positive response to large stimuli and a negative response to small stimuli. Color (black or white) is not relevant. There are two ways of shifting to a new classification of the same set of stimuli. In the upper instance of Figure 13 the response to large stimuli becomes negative without warning, while the response to small stimuli is now positive. Since the responses are interchanged in relation to the initial learning, this is called a *reversal shift*. It is a shift within the same dimension, in this case size.

In contrast, the lower instance in the figure depicts a shift in which a new dimension becomes the basis for choice. Black shapes now have become positive, while white shapes are negative. This is not a complete reversal, since large black stimuli are still positive, and small white stimuli are still negative. However, small black stimuli have changed, as have large white stimuli. This is called a *nonreversal shift* or a shift to a new dimension. If the shift is considered in terms of stimulus-response connections, only half of the old connections still are correct, while half are wrong. In contrast, all of the old stimulus-response relationships change in the reversal shift.

Which is learned faster, the reversal or the nonreversal shift? In terms of stimulus-response connections there are fewer to be relearned in the case of nonreversal shifts, so perhaps these should be learned faster than the reversal shifts in which all of the connections must be relearned. The

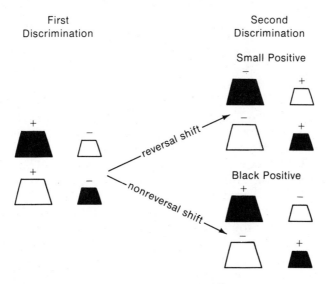

FIGURE 13   Illustration of reversal and nonreversal shifts.

results depend on the kind of organism that is studied. Human adults and older children learn the reversal shift faster than the nonreversal shift, while very young children and rats learn a nonreversal shift faster. How can these divergent findings be reconciled? One possibility is that naive rats and very young children learn by forming individual stimulus-response relationships. Older children do something more complex, perhaps involving mediating responses. They respond to the dimension, as well as to individual values on the dimension. When faced with a reversal shift, older children do not have to relearn responding to the dimension, since it remains the same. When the change involves a new dimension, these older subjects must discover the new dimension that is involved, so more learning is required. The response to a dimension may be a verbal response, easy for older persons but harder for the young. At least part of the difference related to age may be explained in this way.

Selective Attention

From a slightly different point of view, discrimination learning requires that the organism select out and pay attention to a small set of the varied stimuli impinging on its senses. In some cases there is a preliminary observing response as when a person turns his head to look at something. In other situations attention is not as easily observed as head turning, since the receptor orientation is the same whether an organism responds to shape or color. Of course, with a complex shape the eye may move around the perimeter of the figure on first seeing it, but with a familiar shape a brief glance without eye movements is sufficient to provide information as to both shape and color.

What is involved in attending to color as contrasted with shape? It may be a symbolic mediating process, not necessarily dependent on words. It may require rehearsal of some portion of the stimulus complex, a rehearsal that can keep the relevant cues available while one pauses before responding. Sophisticated organisms do this readily, while others may find it difficult to abstract out individual attributes from the whole object. Learning to attend selectively is a part of learning to learn.

Investigations of discrimination learning in children (Zeaman & House, 1963) suggest that selective attention differs in normal and retarded children. Retarded children are slow in finding the relevant cues, but once they discover them, learning may proceed as rapidly as with normals. Figure 14 shows learning curves for groups of children who reached the criterion on a simple discrimination task on different days. The slowest children had a long period of little improvement, but once improvement began, it was rapid.

These data suggest two stages in discrimination learning. The *selection* stage consists of a search for the relevant cues; the *associative* stage involves mastering the individual values of the relevant dimension. The second stage is the easiest part of the learning for retarded children; in fact it may not be appreciably more difficult for them than for normal children.

The initial selection stage could be regarded as a process of hypothesis testing in which the child tries out different hypotheses about the relevant attribute. If an hypothesis is confirmed by correct choices, he continues with the successful hypothesis, but if the hypothesis is disconfirmed, another is tested.

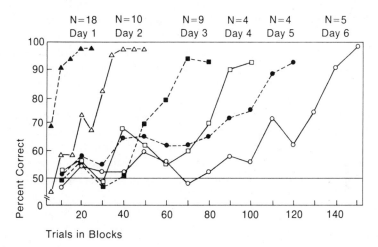

FIGURE 14   Learning curves of groups of subjects reaching the criterion on different days. The number of subjects in each group appears at the top.

From D. Zeaman and B. J. House, The role of attention in retardate discrimination learning. In N. Ellis (Ed.), *Handbook of mental deficiency.* Copyright © 1963 McGraw-Hill Book Company. Used with permission of McGraw-Hill Book Company.

In the selection stage, the number of irrelevant cues is vital in determining rate of learning. The more irrelevant cues there are, the slower the learning. On the other hand, the more relevant dimensions there are, the fewer the errors (Bourne & Haygood, 1961). Added relevant dimensions provide extra cues by which the task can be learned, and the more relevant cues there are relative to irrelevant cues, the faster a useful dimension can be discovered. In the studies of discrimination learning among retarded children (Zeaman & House, 1963), the children learned much more rapidly when three-dimensional objects were the stimuli instead of two-dimensional patterns.

As for the associative stage, this is easy when there are only a few stimuli and responses involved. In simple discrimination experiments with humans, the number of associations required may be so few as to be learned very quickly. There is no difficult associative learning involved here, so the question of whether there is continuity or noncontinuity within the associative stage remains unanswered.

PERCEPTUAL LEARNING

Discrimination learning involves multiple processes: learning a response, discovering the relevant aspect of the stimulus, and associating this relevant cue with the response. Perceptual learning, on the other hand, involves only one of these three processes, namely, learning about the stimulus. Perceptual learning is a change in the ability to obtain information from environmental stimulation (Gibson, 1969). Of course, some response by the subject is required to assess the change objectively, but this response need not be the one that occurred during the perceptual learning; indeed, the learning should be independent of the response involved in its measurement. In order to avoid interaction of perceptual learning with response learning, some simple response is used to reflect perception. For example, the subject can be instructed to compare two stimuli and respond "same" or "different."

One simple situation in which perceptual learning has been studied is the making of psychophysical judgments. In lifting weights, the judgment of differences between weights improves even though no knowledge of results is given. Practice with correction may speed such learning, but improvement can occur without any feedback (Bjorkman & Ottander, 1959). No overt response is learned to a specific weight, so no associative learning is involved. The learning is perceptual interpretation of stimulation.

Distinctive Features

Perceptual learning of the distinctive features of unfamiliar stimuli has been studied through the use of nonsense scribbles (Gibson & Gibson, 1955). Figure 15 illustrates the stimulus material which varied in three dimensions or features: number of coils, horizontal stretching, and right-left orientation. The subjects saw only one scribble at a time, so that the differences were not as obvious as they appear here. A subject was shown one of the scribbles on a card, and then shown a pack of cards (one at a time) in which there were four duplicates of the one shown originally mixed in with a number of differing scribbles. The subject was told to identify the duplicates as they appeared. Erroneous identifications decreased as the experiment continued, even though knowledge of results was not provided. Adults learned faster than children, and older children learned faster than young children. The difference between a test stimulus and the original stimulus involved one, two, or three features, and the number of errors that were made was related to the degree of difference between the stimuli. The more features on which two stimuli differed, the less likely it was that the stimuli were judged identical.

In studies with adults, the recognition of aircraft benefited from instruction in the features that were relevant for their differentiation

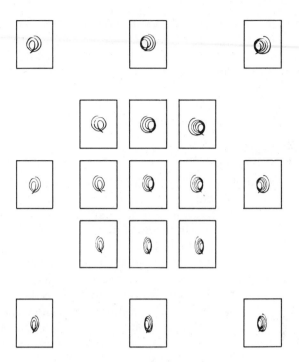

FIGURE 15   Nonsense figures differing in three dimensions.

(Gagné & Gibson, 1947). This was more effective than attempting to learn to recognize aircraft on the basis of the whole shape. Thus, one view of perceptual learning maintains that learning about stimuli is basically the discovery of *distinctive features* of the stimuli.

Coding Responses

Another aspect of perceptual learning emphasizes the acquisition of coding responses to stimuli. For instance, cues acquire distinctiveness when labels are learned for them (Miller & Dollard, 1941). In becoming familiar with the nonsense scribbles of Figure 15, the subjects were heard to use words such as "curl" and "spiral." The availability of labels is related to age, so the greater success of older individuals may be accounted for in part by their greater use of verbal-coding responses. On the other hand, coding responses need not be limited to verbal responses by humans; they could involve other kinds of responses in nonverbal animals. In either case, coding responses can be helpful in interpreting a new situation, regardless of what new response might be demanded.

In criticism of this approach, it has been noted that unless differences among the stimuli can be recognized, distinctive labels cannot be applied accurately. In other words, differentiation of the stimuli must precede the production of any coding response, and not the reverse.

On the other hand, the importance of labels should not be underestimated, since once labels have been associated with distinctive features, the labels can act as a selective mechanism in perception. Having a label in one's repertoire can result in looking for features to correspond to the label and facilitating classification of new stimuli.

Complex Perception

When it comes to perception involving language, the approaches just mentioned are not sufficient to account for the facts. Both visual recognition of printed material and auditory speech perception are complex skills. Analysis of speech in terms of distinctive features is enlightening, but the features of individual speech sounds merge into larger units of meaning which have their own characteristics. Beyond these units there are even larger contexts which influence perception.

In the perception of speech, phrases can be identified when individual words cannot. Pollack & Pickett (1963) recorded the speech of subjects at one session and played it back at another session using apparatus which permitted presentation of different lengths of speech sequences. Speech as limited as a single word could be played back and compared with perception of longer sequences. The subjects found it difficult to identify individual words, but when longer sequences were played back perception was accurate.

In everyday life the individual analyzes sequences of considerable length. Taking reading as an example, reading is organized so that the skilled reader does not read letters or even individual words but can skim phrases and sentences for meaning. Small components can be omitted, and the message will be perceived due to the high redundancy of the English language. Part of the skill consists in coordinating movements of the eyes. Reading requires one to put together a string of looks, called *fixations,* during which the eye is stationary. During the movements of the eye there is no reading for all practical purposes, and the greatest proportion of time in reading is spent on fixations. As a child becomes a skilled reader, the number of fixations per line decreases, and the time spent in each fixation decreases as does the number of backward (regressive) movements over material already covered. Movement from one fixation to another takes a fraction of a second, and over 90 percent of reading time may be spent in fixations.

The most important components of reading skill are not muscle movements; what goes on during fixations is most significant. Grammatical cues assist the reader, and knowledge of what has gone before prepares for what is to come. Skilled reading has been likened to a sampling process in which visual stimuli are integrated with what the reader knows about language and about the particular subject matter (Brown, 1970). This processing depends not only on the size of the reader's vocabulary but on his ability to organize and grasp phrases.

Sensory Substitution

Dramatic illustrations of perceptual learning are provided by attempts to enable the blind to perceive objects at a distance by means of tactile stimulation on the skin (Bach y Rita, 1972). A small lens mounted on spectacles can pick up light energy which can be transformed by a matrix of vibratory stimulators on the abdomen. Blind persons can learn to interpret these relatively crude patterns on the skin, and telephones, pitchers, and other objects can be identified after practice. Three-dimensional interpretations can be made from this two-dimensional spatial pattern; subjects have been observed to duck as an object approaches them.

The learning in this case transfers from practice on one part of the skin to tests on some other part of the skin. The blind have been reading by means of touch for many years, and auditory cues have been used to orient the blind in walking about. Sounds from tapping canes bounce back from objects in their paths. Perceiving the world is a function of learning to interpret whatever cues can be detected by one's sensory organs.

5

Verbal Learning

The symbolic activity of the human is largely carried out by means of words and numbers. These symbols have standardized meanings for adults of the same community, and the use of symbols is a social enterprise. One approach to the study of symbols is to conduct conditioning studies using words as stimuli or responses. Another approach investigates learning of lists of words and other verbal items. The findings from such list-learning experiments will be surveyed in the present chapter.

Free-recall learning is the simplest of three major techniques for investigating verbal learning. A list of unrelated words is presented one word at a time, and the learner is instructed to recall, in order, as many words from the list as possible. The list is presented again in a new order, and a second test of recall is given. As trials continue, more and more words can be recalled from the list.

Paired-associate learning involves a list of pairs of verbal items presented one pair at a time. Usually an anticipation technique is used in which one member of a pair is shown as a stimulus with instructions to give the other member as a response. Both members of the pair are then shown together to correct or confirm the subject's response. After going through the list, one pair at a time, the list is presented again in a new order. The technique is similar to that used by students of a foreign language who make up a pack of cards with an English word on one side and its foreign equivalent on the other. One goes through the pack, looking first at a foreign word while trying to supply its English equivalent, and then turning the card over to ascertain the correct response.

In *serial* learning the experimenter deliberately sets out to get his subjects to develop relationships ordering all of the items in the list. The order of the verbal items in the list is constant from trial to trial. Usually the subject attempts to anticipate the next item as he looks at the current item. The presentation of the next item serves both as information about the accuracy of the anticipation, and as a stimulus for the succeeding item. Each item is in turn response and then stimulus, in contrast to paired-associate learning in which stimulus and response functions are separated.

CHARACTERISTICS OF VERBAL ITEMS

Meaningfulness

The use of verbal items as stimuli or responses poses problems for the experimenter because of past learning. Common words have been heard and spoken by adults in many contexts, so that a given word may have acquired many meanings. An unfamiliar word, on the other hand, may or may not produce a response in the individual, depending on whether or not it resembles some more familiar word. Experimenters have attempted to measure the meaningfulness of individual verbal items in objective ways before assembling them for experimental use. Meaningfulness is not determined by a dictionary definition of a term but rather by the complexity of the individual's reaction to the term.

One way to measure meaningfulness is by scaling verbal items in terms of *association value.* Investigators ask subjects to indicate what a letter combination suggests, and then scales are devised in terms of the percent of persons reporting an association. Unfortunately this scaling does not distinguish between words of high or low meaningfulness, since all evoke associations.

Another technique is to count the number of associations to a given verbal item that can be produced in a standard interval, say one minute. Meaningfulness is then defined as the average number of associations for the item in a group of subjects (Noble, 1952). The scale values that this technique produces are shown in Figure 16. Meaningfulness defined in this way refers to the degree to which subjects react to a verbal item.

Does this kind of association value have any relationship to the use of the items in a learning experiment? The results of an experiment dealing with *paired associates* indicate that it does (Cieutat, Stockwell, & Noble,

WORD	m VALUE
gojey	0.99
femur	2.09
argon	3.34
quota	4.68
uncle	6.59
money	8.98

FIGURE 16 Selected two-syllable verbal items ranked in order of increasing mean frequency of continued associations in 60 seconds.

1958). In this experiment graphed in Figure 17 meaningfulness was varied independently for stimulus and response members of the list. In one list both stimuli and responses were of high meaningfulness, while in another list both members of a pair were of low meaningfulness. In the other two lists either stimuli or responses were of high meaningfulness, but not both. The learning was found to proceed most rapidly when both members of a pair were high in meaningfulness. In general, meaningfulness made a bigger difference for responses than for stimuli. Thus, the condition using high-meaningful responses with low-meaningful stimuli resulted in faster learning than the condition having high-meaningful stimuli and low-meaningful responses.

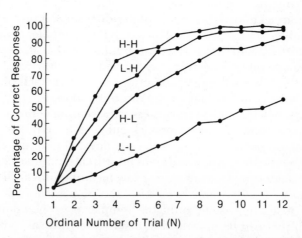

FIGURE 17   Learning curves for four conditions of meaningfulness (*m*): High stimulus *m* and high response *m* (H-H); high stimulus *m* and low response *m* (H-L); low stimulus *m* and high response *m* (L-H); and low stimulus *m* and low response *m* (L-L).

Imagery Value

Another way of classifying words is based on the images they evoke (Paivio, Yuille, & Madigan, 1968). Subjects rated words on a scale ranging from "very easy—image aroused immediately" to "very difficult—image aroused after a long delay or not at all." Difficulty in learning paired-associates was related to ratings on the scale: the higher the imagery rating, the faster the learning. Furthermore, a high imagery rating had a greater effect on stimuli than on responses, which is in contrast to findings with association value.

When imagery rating and association value are measured for the same word, the imagery value and the association value are related to one another, but the effect of imagery is not merely an accompaniment of association value. When sets of items are made equal in average association value, superior learning with high imagery words can still be found. On the other hand it is more difficult to demonstrate differences related to association value independently of imagery. Paivio (1971) considers imagery to be the basic variable underlying association value, at least for concrete words. For abstract words like justice or honesty, verbal processes may be more important than imagery.

Instructions to use visual imagination have produced markedly superior verbal learning (Bower, 1972). Particularly when subjects are instructed to imagine objects interacting together, a high degree of learning may be achieved in a single trial. In contrast, instructions that fail to mention imagery produce much slower learning. An image can bring together individual members of a pair of words into a single unit. Evidence comes from studies in which drawings of two interacting objects were presented (Epstein, Rock, & Zuckerman, 1960), and compared with the two objects drawn apart from each other.

An illustration of a recent study of paired words is seen in Figure 18 (Wollen, Weber, & Lowry, 1972). Four conditions were compared, so that the objects either did or did not interact, and the relationship was either bizarre or not bizarre. Drawings were shown in conjunction with the names of the objects. The conditions in which the objects interacted resulted in much better learning of the pairings. However, contrary to what has sometimes been claimed, it made no difference whether the relationship was bizarre; the important variable was the interaction of the objects.

FREE-RECALL LEARNING

Subjective Organization

Since the subject in a free-recall study is not instructed to recall the words in any particular order, the learning might seem to involve a collection of items without any connections or associations among them. However, Tulving (1962) has identified the reason for improved recall from one trial to the next as subjective organization. Each subject organizes the words and tends to recall groups of words together trial after trial. These stereotyped groupings in recall persist in spite of the changing order of presentation from one trial to the next. Subjects organize the words into larger and larger groups as trials continue. The same number of groups may be recalled as learning progresses, but a group contains more words, and so more words are recalled.

Noninteracting, nonbizarre

Noninteracting, bizarre

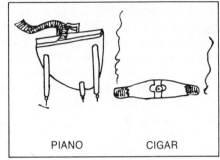

Interacting, nonbizarre

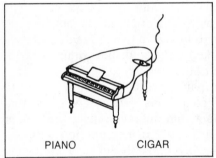

Interacting, bizarre

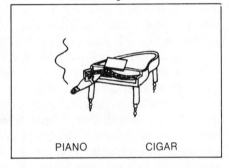

FIGURE 18   Sample materials for four conditions of paired-associate learning.

Part-whole Transfer

Many verbal-learning studies are concerned with the transfer of training of one task to a later task. The effect of previous learning on a new task can be either positive or negative. *Positive transfer* is identified when the later task is performed better than it would have been without the earlier task having been learned. *Negative transfer* refers to inferior performance on a later task due to learning of some previous task.

The importance of subjective organization in free recall was pointed up by a transfer study (Tulving, 1966) in which part of a list was studied for several trials before the complete list was presented. Thus, the transfer in this case was from training on part of a task to learning of the whole task. First, subjects completed several trials on a short list of words; then, half of them learned a longer list which contained no words from the original list. The remaining subjects learned a list of equal length that contained the words from the original list in addition to the new words; thus, these subjects already knew some of the words. Surprisingly, duplication of words in the two lists did not result in a permanent advantage in the learning of the second list. Figure 19 indicates that previous exposure to some of the words was only a temporary advantage. In the long run, the subjects who learned all new words did better than the others.

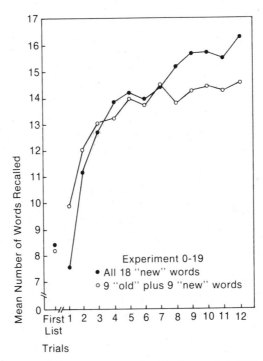

FIGURE 19   Learning curves for two groups of subjects on a list of 18 words. One group (open circles) learned half the list prior to learning the whole list, while the other group (filled circles) learned a previous unrelated list.

These findings suggest that subjects began organizing the words in the first short list. When they were switched to the longer list which included the old list, the organization from the previous learning interfered with organization of the new list. In contrast, with the completely new list, no interference was present.

Hierarchical Organization

Subjective organization can be considered a network of associations linking one word with a number of other words. In some cases, the organization of verbal elements learned in the past takes the form of clearly identifiable hierarchies of terms. We learn classes of labels in school and at home that become standard for a particular culture. For example, study the hierarchy of minerals shown in Figure 20, a set of terms which was used in a free-recall experiment (Bower, Clark, Lesgold, & Winzenz, 1969). Large differences in free recall were found which were related to how the words were presented. For the first group of subjects, all of the terms in the figure were shown for four trials, but with random placement of individual words. For the second group, only words from Levels 1 and 2 were presented on the first trial, while words from Levels 1–3 were presented on the second trial. Finally, on the last two trials all of the words were presented. The second group of subjects learned the class names before learning the instances of a class. In spite of the fact that Level-4 words had not been presented as many times in this group, they were learned much faster than in the random group. Organization, related to past learning, was more important than sheer frequency of presentation.

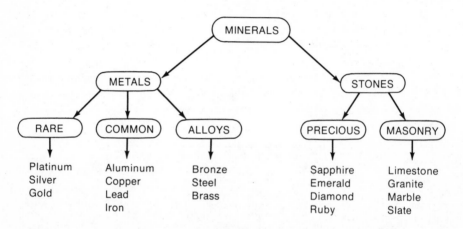

FIGURE 20   A four-level hierarchy of concepts.

PAIRED-ASSOCIATE LEARNING

Associative Component

Paired-associate learning lends itself to interpreting verbal skills in terms of individual stimuli and their associated responses. Presumably a list of pairs has a number of independent associations, and an average over the pairs for each trial of an experiment should give an indication of the course of learning for a typical pair. Learning curves typically give a picture of gradual improvement, and a traditional interpretation is that each repetition adds a little bit to the associative strength linking one member of the pair to the other.

This interpretation of verbal learning has been challenged by a number of recent experiments since averaging may hide the true shape of the learning curve for individual items. The graph in Figure 21 shows how averaging items which were learned suddenly could give the appearance of a gradually increasing learning curve. The sudden learning could take place on any trial, including the first trial, whenever the subject discovered some mnemonic device for linking the pairs. The finding that images may mediate between members of a pair gives general support to such an interpretation, as do findings that subjects use words as mediators (Montague, 1972).

A type of experiment specifically designed to test for sudden learning of individual pairs used a *dropout technique* in one condition. Instead of keeping all of the pairs in the list until they were learned, as is usually done, pairs were dropped out if they were missed and replaced with new pairs. Strangely enough, the dropping out of pairs didn't slow subjects' learning (Rock, 1957). If a pair could be replaced with a new pair without handicapping the learner, nothing had been learned about the dropped pair. Hence learning must be all or none, occurring suddenly on some unpredictable trial.

One difficulty in accepting this conclusion is that pairs that are missed tend to be more difficult than the average pair which replaces them. The learner may end up with an easier list than the one he started with which might counterbalance any learning lost by replacement of partially

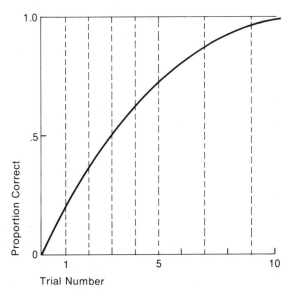

FIGURE 21   The solid line represents a learning curve averaged over individual pairs which were learned suddenly. Absence of dashed line indicated nothing was learned on that particular trial.

learned pairs. In support of this criticism are findings that the initial list does tend to be harder to learn than the final list (Underwood, Rehula, & Keppel, 1962).

Another approach is to find new ways of averaging to get a better indication of the course of learning. For instance, instead of averaging over all items from the beginning, one could start from the point of the last error, lining up items from this point and average backward for several trials. The sudden learning interpretation would imply that on the trials before the last error for an individual item, the learning curve should be flat at the chance level of responding. On the other hand, if items are learned gradually, there should be improvement before the last error.

Backward learning curves do show some improvement prior to the last error except in special cases. An exception is the case where only two response alternatives are used with a number of stimulus members in a list. In this case the backward learning curve is flat, hovering at the 50-percent level. With more than two response alternatives, there tends to be some improvement prior to the last error, although there still is a substantial improvement from the trial before to the trial after the last error.

A number of factors may contribute to these findings, and a serious consideration of all of them is beyond the scope of this book. However, one plausible explanation is that some pairs are learned slowly in laborious rote fashion, while others are learned by discovering mnemonic aids. The backward learning curve averages over both cases.

Evidence of continued learning even after errors cease is found in the latencies of responses after the last error. Time to recall decreases as the trials continue. There is improvement of some kind even though a big boost in the learning occurred at some earlier point.

Response Learning

The discussion of the previous section has ignored any learning other than the associative component. It assumed that the stimuli and responses were both familiar integrated units so that they needed only to be linked in some manner. If stimuli and responses are unfamiliar, then learning should not be expected on a single trial.

There is more to paired-associate learning than the formation of associations. *Response learning* is also involved to a greater or lesser degree, depending on the kind of response that is involved. As trials continue in a paired-associate task, the subject learns the responses without being able to assign all of them to their appropriate stimuli. This is reflected in the kind of errors that are made, since responses that are not from the list no longer occur; errors are misplaced responses from other pairs. If the response to be learned is not a familiar organized unit such as a word, the integration of a collection of letters may be required. With nonsense items of low meaningfulness, response learning is slow.

Stimulus Learning

In addition, *stimulus learning* is frequently required in paired-associate learning. Stimulus learning may involve perceptual learning, and the discussion of the previous chapter applies here. In addition to learning to perceive unfamiliar stimuli, the learner may select a single aspect of the stimulus for his response. This is one reason why meaningfulness affects the response side of paired-associate learning more than the stimulus side. The learner must give the response as the experimenter defines it, thereby selecting any aspect of the stimulus that is useful. If all first letters of the stimuli are different from one another, the learner may attend only to first letters and simplify his task. Of course, if stimuli are highly similar and have many letters in common with one another, then integration of the whole stimulus into a unit may be required. Learning is slower in this latter case.

Perceptual learning of verbal stimuli can be seen in visual recognition of letters of varying degrees of organization, as in comparison of unrelated letters versus words versus phrases. Many more letters can be recognized in a brief glance if they constitute words than if they are unrelated to one another. Even more letters can be reported when words are organized into phrases.

The three individual components—response learning, stimulus learning, and associative learning—can be varied independently of one another in the same experiment (McGuire, 1961). Stimuli can be made to vary in similarity; highly similar stimuli make learning difficult, and low similarity stimuli permit easy stimulus differentiation. Second, the responses can be unrelated and thus require integration, or they can be unified permitting rapid response learning. Finally, both stimuli and responses can vary directly on the same dimension, or the relationships can be mixed up, which slows learning. Thus, the individual components determine how difficult it is to learn the total task.

Transfer Effects

Learning of a second verbal task usually goes faster than the first task. In part this is a *general transfer* effect unrelated to the particular verbal items used in the second task. Subjects learn the general procedures involved, adapt to irrelevant distractions in the laboratory, and develop techniques to complete their task. In addition to this general transfer, *specific transfer* effects have been identified; they are related to identical or similar verbal elements in two successive tasks. In evaluating specific transfer of training effects, the experimental design will almost invariably permit measurement of the amount of general transfer in the situation.

Transfer studies in verbal learning have accumulated labels which permit quick designation of the particular paradigm being used. Thus, the control paradigm against which other transfer effects are compared is referred to as an A - B, C - D design; that is, all of the elements in the first task are different from those in the second. When the second list requires that new responses be learned to the original stimuli from the first list, the designation is A - B, A - D. Since the term designating the first list is always the same, a condition can be referred to by the composition of its second list.

Transfer can be positive or negative; previous learning can facilitate later learning, or it can hinder it. In the A - D paradigm, the transfer is negative when compared with the control condition as can be seen in Figure 22. However, the amount of negative transfer produced is a function of degree of learning of the first list. With increased learning of the first list, transfer becomes more negative up to a point, and with high learning of the first list there is actually a decrease in the amount of negative transfer (Postman, 1962).

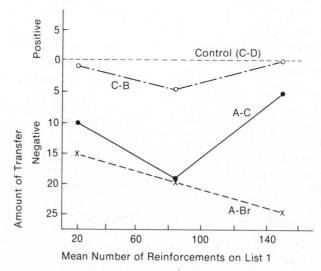

FIGURE 22   Amounts of negative transfer as measured by the differences between the control condition (C-D) and each of the experimental conditions in mean number correct in ten trials on the second list.

Negative transfer is clearly seen with an A - B$_r$ design, in which both stimuli and responses are the same from first to second list, but the pairings are rearranged. Transfer becomes increasingly negative the greater the degree of learning of the first list. In spite of the fact that one would expect positive contributions due to stimulus and response learning being transferred, the negative aspect of the associative changes outweighs other considerations.

In a design in which the same responses are common to both lists but new stimuli are introduced (C - B), learning is easier than in either of the two paradigms just considered. In this case another factor enters in—the meaningfulness of the responses. With low-meaningfulness responses, there is marked positive transfer with the C - B design. However, with high meaningfulness responses, performance is little better than the control condition, so there is neither positive nor negative transfer (Jung, 1963).

SERIAL LEARNING

The importance of serial learning is not easily overestimated. Children learn the elements of the number system, the letters of the alphabet, the days of the week, and many other serial structures. These structures enable individuals to orient themselves in time, as well as to make calculated judgments involving the manipulation of numbers. Such elementary structures may be the building blocks for complex cognitive skills.

Effective Stimulus

It may seem clear that serial learning involves a chain of connections or associations from beginning to end of a set of verbal items. However, this conception is too simple, as has been demonstrated experimentally. Consider a transfer experiment (Young, 1962) in which a serial task is learned, followed by a paired-associate task. The pairs in the second task are taken from adjacent positions in the serial list. Presumably the second list should be easy to learn, since connections between pairs should have been formed during the previous serial learning. However, there is only a small advantage in having learned the previous list. The total number of trials to learn is not lessened by the serial learning. What then is the effective stimulus in serial learning if it is not the preceding item?

The explanation depends on the additional cues that support recall in the serial task. Position in presentation is one such cue. There is an identifiable beginning as well as an end to a serial task, but in the paired-associate task the order changes from trial to trial. The first item can be identified in serial learning, and so can the last. Position learning may particularly aid the learning of the early and late items. When the error-position curve (see Figure 23) is examined, it can be seen that the ends of the list have been learned faster than the middle.

Another cue that may be used in serial learning is a combination of previous items; the stimulus for recall can include two or three items. In contrast, the changing order of pairs in paired-associate learning precludes any consistent stimulus of this kind.

One variation of paired-associate learning has some characteristics of serial learning. The stimulus members of the pairs are members of an ordered set, for instance, the numbers one to ten (Ebenholtz, 1972). Even

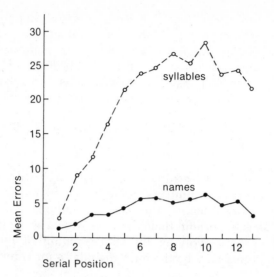

FIGURE 23   Serial-position curves for two kinds of verbal items—nonsense syllables and familiar names.

though the pairs are reordered from trial to trial, a typical serial position curve can be seen if the pairs are graphed in order of their stimuli, 1–10. Pairs at the ends of the scale are learned with the fewest errors, while the most frequently missed pairs have stimuli from the middle of the range. The structure of the set of stimuli produces an effect on the learner in spite of the absence of constant order in presentation.

Grammatical Structure

When the grammatical cues of English are introduced into serial learning, rate of learning increases. Epstein (1962) had subjects learn serial material in which the individual items were nonsense, yet they possessed grammatical characteristics. Figure 24 illustrates the nonsensical material that included some segments resembling grammatical cues. Learning when grammatical cues were present was faster than when these cues were eliminated or the order was random. In comparison, phrase structure contributes to the learning of sentences, and meaningful prose is still easier to learn. In English prose, many cues are available, and imagery may be used to support recall.

The relationship of grammatical structure to learning also was investigated by Johnson (1965). Subjects learned sentences as responses to digits, and transitional error probabilities (TEP) between successive words in each sentence were investigated. The *transitional error probability* refers to the conditional probability that a response is recalled correctly given that the preceding response was correct. TEP's reflected the phrase structure of the sentence; they were higher at the boundaries of phrases.

NONSENSE ITEMS
Grammatical   The glers um cligs wur vasing un seping a rad moovly
Nongrammatical   cligs seping a wur rad un moovly glers the un vasing

MEANINGFUL ITEMS
Grammatical   Helping walls met eating trees from noisy poor lines
Nongrammatical   noisy trees walls from lines helping eating poor met

FIGURE 24   Examples of learning materials used in a study of the effect of grammatical structure on learning.

The phrases tended to be recalled as units, and subjects were likely to recall the whole unit if they recalled the first word, although errors were not uniform within units. Thus, in a sentence such as "The tall boy saved the dying woman," the highest TEP was for the transition from "boy" to "saved" which, of course, marks the major division of the sentence into subject and predicate.

Thus, serial learning is more complex than a chaining of associations. In serial learning, the learner forms a structure, and the sequence becomes a whole with identifiable positions marking the beginning and the end. It may be compared to a familiar word which is a serial list of letters that has been well learned and functions as a unit with characteristics of its own.

The ancient Greeks had a trick for learning the order of a series of items. They used a familiar building with many nooks and crannies as a structure in which to store a series. The aspiring orator was instructed to remember the points in his speech by walking through such a building in his imagination. Each point in the speech was imagined as placed in a successive part of the building. Remembering involved a sequence of images placed in order by the familiar structure, and the same structure was used over and over again in many speeches.

Contemporary experimenters have studied the effect of teaching subjects a spatial map of a street containing business places. After learning the map, subjects attempt to associate a list of words with positions along the street (Crovitz, 1969). Subjects perform well using such mnemonic devices, although it has been questioned whether bizarre images are necessary or any more effective than some verbal mnemonics (Johnson, 1972).

6

Retention

A new dimension is introduced into learning by considering that information available earlier may no longer be recalled. Look up a new number in the telephone directory, dial the number and talk to your party, and then try to remember what the number was. You may find that you forgot the number while you talked on the phone. Laboratory studies of remembering follow the general outline of this example. Information is presented to a subject, an interval filled with distracting activity follows, and then a test of the information is given. The longer the interval since the information was processed, the poorer the retention of that information. Variables such as the kind of activity during the retention interval, the kind of test that is given, and the degree of learning—these all influence retention and its complement, forgetting.

A set of retention curves in Figure 25 shows forgetting over short intervals of time (Peterson & Peterson, 1959). The information in this experiment consisted of three consonants which together lacked meaning. The distracting activity during the retention interval consisted of counting backward from a three-digit number, an activity assumed to minimize any tendency for the subject to rehearse during the retention interval. The test at the end of the interval required the subject to speak the letters in their original order. The retention curves are average proportions recalled in a number of tests for each of a group of subjects. Although the three letters were recalled with high accuracy right after presentation, a considerable amount of forgetting occurred within a few seconds. Fewer presentations were forgotten when the subject rehearsed them before starting to count backward. The more time spent in processing, the greater was the accuracy of recall of the information. The downward trend of the curves indicates that the longer the interval filled with distracting activity, the more the forgetting. Of course, if the tests had been scored without regard to order of the letters, each of the curves would have been somewhat higher, indicating that requirements of the test can make a difference.

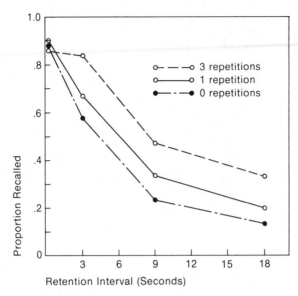

FIGURE 25   Short-term retention after 0, 1, or 3 repetitions.

INFORMATION PROCESSING

The most important factor influencing retention is the amount and type of processing of information prior to the beginning of the retention interval. For example, if a list of paired-associates was not completely learned, it cannot be completely recalled after an interval. Even when recall is 100 percent accurate immediately after learning, later recall depends on the nature of the original processing. In the experiment discussed earlier (see Figure 25) recall right after presentation was about 90 percent accurate; after 18 seconds of distracting activity, recall depended on the amount of rehearsal given the letters.

Three kinds of storage play an important role in remembering: sensory memory, working memory, and long-term memory. It is not possible to point to three parts of the nervous system which correspond to these terms; rather they are related to the degree of information processing. A schematic diagram of the interaction of these three aspects of memory is shown in Figure 26. Sensory memory maintains information in a form related to the sensory organ which detected the information. This is temporary storage, and information is soon lost if it is not processed further. In working memory, rehearsal maintains selected information while it is coded into a form which can be stored over long-term intervals. Long-term memory provides codes which transform sensory signals into abstract forms (usually verbal) so that information can be rehearsed in working memory. In addition long-term memory furnishes information and techniques of processing that permit the activities of the working memory. Finally, long-term memory includes motor habits which aid the output of information, as well as networks of interrelated concepts that comprise our knowledge of the world.

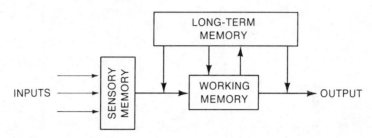

FIGURE 26   Three aspects of memory associated with information processing.

Sensory Memory

Remembering a spoken message has sometimes been compared to listening to an echo (Waugh & Norman, 1965). Specific acoustic properties are remembered, and errors are frequently related to the way messages sound. Phonemes, the smallest units of speech sound that make a difference in distinguishing one word from another, are easily confused when they have acoustic features in common, such as "b" and "t." Strings of letters that are highly similar in sound to one another are harder to recall after short retention intervals than less similar sounding letter combinations.

Visual stimulation leaves images which are even shorter than the echo after an auditory message. Visual images can be measured with the aid of a tachistoscope, a device for presenting brief glimpses of visual stimuli. When three rows of letters are exposed simultaneously, the subject is unable to recall them if the number of letters exceeds his memory span. However, a partial recall can be obtained by introducing a tone which indicates whether the top, middle, or bottom row of letters should be recalled. If this signal is given immediately after the exposure, the subject is able to report the letters in the specified row with a high degree of accuracy. If a short delay occurs, performance is poorer even though no other activity occurs during the interval.

For a brief time after exposure, a visual image is still available to the subject. Under normal circumstances an image lasts only a fraction of a second, but if the field is dark before and after the exposure, it may last several seconds. Like an echo, a visual image is subject to interference by similar sensory events (Sperling, 1963).

An intriguing sensory effect arises after visual presentations of strings of letters which are read silently. Errors in recall after visual presentations often are similar in sound to the correct letter. Furthermore, sets of letters that sound similar to one another are not remembered as well as sets in which the letters sound less similar, even after a visual presentation. The sensory cues must be added during processing by the readers as they rehearse to themselves. These similarity effects can be eliminated by having subjects articulate an irrelevant task while viewing the presentation (Peterson & Johnson, 1971). Sets of similar sounding letters are then remembered with the same accuracy as less similar sounding sets. The sensory features arising during silent articulation are much like acoustic features, and like them may be useful for retention to the extent that they are distinctive. If they are not distinctive, they may hinder recall.

Working Memory

In addition to providing articulatory cues and maintaining information, rehearsal is one step in the processing of information for long-term storage. However, there is a reciprocal relationship in which, at least in the case of verbal rehearsal, the conversion of sensory features into speech requires the use of habits of long standing. Before a letter is rehearsed, it is converted from auditory or visual signals into abstract elements of language. Similarly, words must be recognized before they can be rehearsed in any meaningful way.

Once information is in verbal form so that it can be rehearsed, the processing proceeds. The action of the working memory in relation to long-term storage was seen in a free-recall study in which the amount of rehearsal during presentation of a list was observed (Rundus & Atkinson, 1970). The subjects were instructed to rehearse out loud, and this rehearsal was recorded and later analyzed. The amount of rehearsal observed for different positions in the list is shown in Figure 27, as is the proportion of items recalled. Subjects rehearsed items in direct relation to their proximity to the beginning of the list—the first items getting the most rehearsal and the last items the least. Number of words recalled was directly related to amount of rehearsal except for the last few positions. These results reflect different levels of processing of items in the list. The early and middle positions reflect long-term storage of items in direct proportion to the amount of rehearsal given them. In the final portion of the curve, recall is facilitated by the contribution of the working memory as well as sensory storage.

Recall in the final portion of the serial-position curve for free recall is related to mode of presentation (Murdock & Walker, 1969). Auditory presentations are recalled better than visual presentations for a few seconds after presentation. However, mode of presentation does not ordinarily affect the middle or beginning of the list. This is an indication

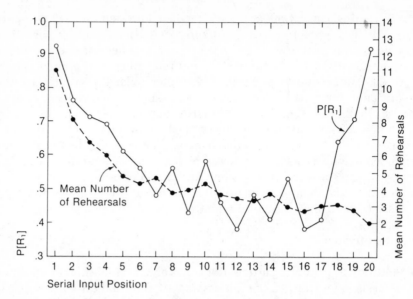

FIGURE 27   Probability of recalling an item compared to the mean number of rehearsals given an item, as a function of serial position.

that sensory characteristics are involved in recalling recent presentations but not earlier ones. Further support for this interpretation of the strong recency effect in free recall comes from the shape of the serial-position curve when a delay filled with distracting activity occurs before the test for recall. Figure 28 indicates that the graphs of immediate and delayed recall are very similar except for the final portion of the curves. Short-term sensory cues are no longer available after a delay, and the recall that occurs is based on higher-level storage induced by rehearsal.

Coding is of basic importance in processing information so that it may be more readily retained. Consider the scheme illustrated in Figure 29 which can be used to improve the recall of sequences of binary digits. Binary or two-valued digits are grouped by threes, and each possible combination is assigned a label; the sequence "010" is called "2" for instance. By means of a label three digits become one chunk, and the labels can be stored instead of the binary digits. When recalling the sequence, the label can be decoded back into binary digits, and the original sequence is reproduced.

Well-practiced subjects can remember almost three times as many binary digits after a single presentation if the code is used (Miller, 1956). Only a limited number of chunks can be stored in the working memory, but with the code each chunk or label represents three digits. This particular code is useful for programming computers, since the information in a digital computer is stored in binary form.

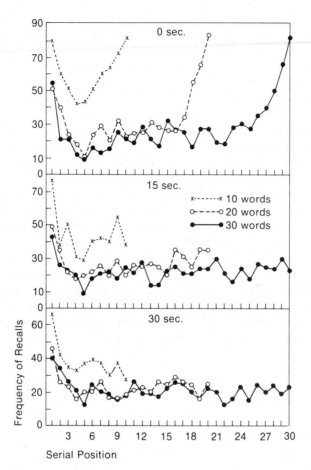

FIGURE 28   Serial position curves of free recall for lists of three lengths after delays of 0, 15, or 30 seconds.

BINARY	OCTAL LABEL
000	0
001	1
010	2
011	3
100	4
101	5
110	6
111	7

FIGURE 29   An octal code for binary digits.

Literate individuals have learned to code combinations of letters into units called words. The three-letter combinations of the Peterson et al. (1959) experiment (see Figure 25) did not form a word. When three letters making up a word are used, retention is much better, even after a single presentation without time for rehearsal (Murdock, 1961). Retention of a word is as good as retention of a single letter. On the other hand, three letters are remembered about as well as three words after equivalent delays filled with distracting activity. The important factor is the number of integrated chunks which constitute the presentation. The more unrelated chunks there are to remember—whether letters or words—the faster they are forgotten.

Can sensory information be rehearsed without coding it into words? The effect of instructions to use visual imagery in verbal learning, and the relevance of imagery ratings to learning, suggest that sensory characteristics are not limited to sensory memory, but play a role in working memory and long-term memory as well. It is difficult to investigate sensory rehearsal apart from the readily available verbal habits of the human; even nonsense figures may be coded into words. Experiments with pure tones suggest that sensory attributes of a simple kind can be rehearsed, and that these are abstracted out of the total sensory input and maintained at the expense of other sensory attributes (Kinchla, 1973).

Long-term Memory

A prominent component of long-term memory in the human is the memory required to use language. In addition to codes needed to convert acoustic signals into speech sounds, long-term memory is organized in such a way that language has meaning. Semantic memory supplies meaning to collections of words, and objective evidence of its existence can be found in the ability of the individual to supply a paraphrase of a sentence that he heard previously. Semantic memory is memory for the meaning of a complex input, and it suggests storage of information at a more abstract level than the storage of particular words.

Semantic memory has been represented as an organization of interrelated words, sometimes in a hierarchical structure as depicted in Figure 30. Terms at one level of the hierarchy are instances of a higher-level term, and the structure resembles the branching of a tree. Networks of concepts of this kind are called into service not only when memory is tested directly, but also when an individual attempts to understand language.

Precise details about the exact words used in a story or the individual sounds of a phrase may be lost, yet the basic meaning may be retained. Semantic memory is involved, and irrelevant characteristics drop out. For example, forgetting of trivial words and the retention of meaning is well documented (Sachs, 1967). Furthermore, Bransford & Franks (1971) have found that individual sentences combined into a structured whole in

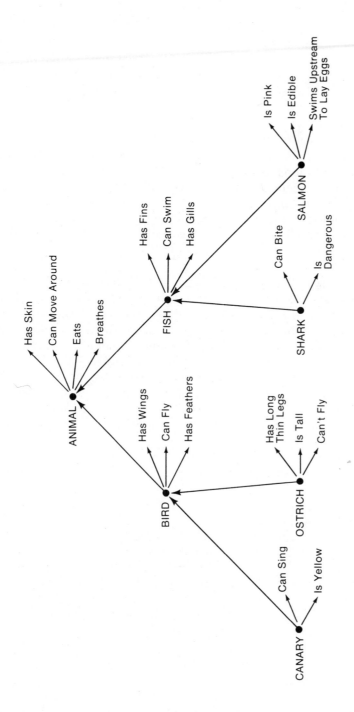

FIGURE 30   A hypothetical memory structure for a 3-level hierarchy.

memory so that subjects knew details of the total pattern of information but might not recognize the exact sentences by which the information was obtained. Subjects reported recognition of material which fitted the total story but which was not actually presented in that form. There was false recognition of sentences, so that the greater the amount of information in the test sentence, the more certain subjects were that they were given that particular sentence.

An aspect of memory that has been contrasted to semantic memory is episodic memory (Tulving, 1972). The latter is memory for events as such, rather than information related to language. Episodic memory refers to the capability to recall events of an autobiographical nature, as, for instance, in recalling events leading up to breakfast, or even memory for a list of syllables presented in an experiment. Although such information may be stored for long periods if it is well rehearsed, episodic memory tends to endure for shorter periods than semantic memory since it is less organized.

Syntactic rules, hypotheses, strategies, and various kinds of language combinations have all been stored for long-term availability. In addition there are images and other nonlanguage components that may endure over long periods of time. The presence of images which can be retrieved after long intervals indicates that sensory cues do not always fade away after a brief interval. Sensory cues can be rehearsed and coded in nonverbal form. Ask someone how many windows there are in his bedroom, and he may ask you to wait while he visualizes the room and counts the windows. Sound patterns also can be stored for long-term availability. In some instances, individuals report that they can remember how things feel.

Incidental Versus Instructed Learning

Information processing is affected by the kind of instructions the learner receives. For instance, one group of subjects can be instructed to learn some verbal materials in order to prepare for a later test, while another group is exposed to the materials on the pretext that they are performing some nonlearning task. As might be expected, there is better retention of the materials for subjects instructed to learn. However, under some circumstances the differences between instructed learning and incidental learning is not great; the critical factor is what the subjects do in relation to the materials (Postman, 1964). There is no magical effect that accompanies a subject's intention to learn; learning will be a function of the processing.

One way to lessen differences between incidental and instructed learning is to restrict the amount of time available for instructed learners to to do more than the incidental learners. The incidental learners are exposed to the learning materials through an orienting task, such as finding numbers on a sheet of paper and checking them. If this orienting task must be performed at a fast rate and if both incidental and instructed learners perform the task, the incidental learners may do as well as the instructed learners on a later retention task for the numbers (Neimark & Saltzman, 1953). With a slow rate of performance on the orienting task, the instructed learners put the extra time to use in memorizing the numbers.

The nature of the orienting task is critical in determining how much the incidental learners acquire. In one study (Rosenberg & Schiller, 1971) subjects were given sentences with differing kinds of orienting tasks. Some subjects were told to estimate the number of letters in each sentence without attempting to count them. Other subjects were told to rate the familiarity of the sentence, a task requiring semantic processing of the sentence. In neither case were these subjects told that they would be tested on recall of the sentence, yet incidental learning was found for both groups. Little incidental learning occurred for the letter-estimation condition, while with the familiarity rating condition recall was virtually as good as for a third group of subjects instructed to memorize the sentences. Thus, the low-level processing involving estimating number of letters did not produce substantial learning, whereas the orienting task requiring semantic processing produced a high degree of learning.

An intriguing contrast to instructed learning is obtained when learners are instructed to forget. Learners are told to forget a task, and then a test on that task is given unexpectedly at the end of the experimental session. The instructed forgetters do not recall as well as control subjects who were not given this deceptive treatment. One interpretation of these findings is that one can erase material that has been learned if he is so motivated. However, a more plausible interpretation is that the instructions affect the subjects' processing of the learning materials (Bjork, 1972). The directions to forget must be given before the coding or rehearsal of the material to be forgotten has occurred; if instructions to forget follow the acquisition stage of an experiment, there is little directed forgetting. The instructions reduce the motivation of subjects to process material, rather than inducing them to erase what has been learned. Permanent storage of information requires rehearsal and coding, so if the individual is not motivated to engage in such processing, he forgets. Instructions to forget before the processing takes place reduce the learner to the status of an incidental learner.

INTERFERENCE AND FORGETTING

Granted that extent of processing is of primary importance for remembering, what causes forgetting of information that has been learned to some specific degree? It is not enough to say that we forget because time passes, since time in itself does not make things happen; processes that occur in time produce changes. Iron does not rust because of the passage of time; chemical reactions occur during a period of time which produce rusting. What is it that happens during time that produces forgetting?

Retroactive Interference

Behavioral events that intervene between learning and recall are a primary contributor to forgetting. New learning can have a negative effect on old learning; this is *retroactive interference.*

From one point of view almost anything you might do during a retention interval could produce interference and hence result in forgetting. However, the similarity of the intervening activity to original learning is important. In the study of retroactive interference, experimenters generally give subjects a task during a retention interval that minimizes rehearsal of the original learning. But apart from rehearsal, tasks similar to the original learning events increase the amount of interference.

An experiment designed to measure *retroactive interference* is outlined in Figure 31. Two tasks, A and B, are learned in succession, after which memory for the first task (A) is tested. The control group learn task A, after which they do something irrelevant, instead of learning task B. If the subjects with the intervening learning task (B) recall less of the first task (A) than do the control subjects, retroactive interference has occurred.

GROUP I	Learn A	Learn B	Test A
GROUP II	Learn A	Rest	Test A

FIGURE 31   Design of an experiment to test for retroactive interference.

Similarity of the intervening event (task B) can be divided into stimulus and response components. Similarity between stimuli may mean visual similarity if nonsense forms are the stimuli, or it may be a semantic similarity if words are used. With nonsense syllables, similarity often is determined by the number of letters which syllables have in common. Over retention intervals of only a few seconds, similarity can be measured by the number of speech sounds messages have in common. Thus, similarity can be assessed along many dimensions.

Similarity has a differential effect, depending on whether stimuli or responses are under consideration. When responses are different, the more similar the stimuli are to one another, the more the forgetting. When stimuli are the same, the more similar the responses to one another, the less the forgetting.

In addition to similarity, the degree of learning of the second task influences the amount of retroactive interference. Forgetting of task A increases with the number of trials spent on task B, at least up to a point. With very high degrees of learning of the second task, retroactive interference levels off and may even decrease a bit.

What is interference? One interpretation is that the new responses being learned compete with the responses from the previous learning. Interference as competition is illustrated in a study by Briggs (1954) in which the relative strength of first-list responses was compared with second-list responses during learning and retention. The task required learning of paired-associates in an A - B, A - D design. Modified free-recall tests were inserted at various points in addition to the usual measures. The instructions on these tests were to give the first response to a given stimulus that a subject thought of regardless of which list it came from. Figure 32 shows how the strength of the two competing responses associated with the same stimulus changed in relation to one another. During first-list learning, appropriate responses from the first list increased with trials. During learning of the second list, first-list responses decreased in frequency while the second-list responses increased. Rest intervals of varying lengths of time were inserted between the end of the second list and the beginning of the relearning of the first list. As these intervals increased, subjects were less and less likely to recall the second-list response. Thus, the relative strength of the two competing responses changed spontaneously over time.

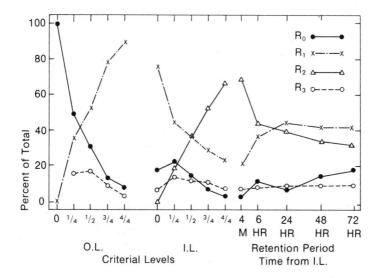

FIGURE 32 Modified free recall tests of competing responses during original learning (A-B), during second-list learning (A-D), and after a retention interval.

The graph in Figure 32 may remind the reader of the eyelid-conditioning graph (see Figure 4), which showed an increase in strength of the conditioned response following a rest interval. The increase was called spontaneous recovery in conditioning, and the parallel phenomenon in verbal learning has led to the hypothesis that extinction or unlearning of the first-list responses occurs during the learning of the second list. The rest interval then permits spontaneous recovery.

One aspect of the verbal learning data, however, has no counterpart in the conditioning data. At the beginning of relearning, subjects are able to produce the appropriate first-list response if so instructed with a higher frequency than is reflected in the free-recall data. Even if the second-list response occurred first in free recall, subjects are still able to give the first-list response in a substantial number of cases.

Retroactive interference may involve more than competition of responses at recall. When the learner is encouraged to give the responses to a given stimulus from both the first and second list, many responses from the first list are not remembered after learning the second list. Figure 33 graphs this kind of experiment, again using the A - B, A - D paradigm (Barnes & Underwood, 1959). The more trials given on the second list, the fewer were the first-list responses that could be recalled.

The inability to recall immediately after second-list learning does not mean that the first-list associations have been lost permanently. Not only do some responses become available with the passage of time (spontaneous recovery), but they are revealed when multiple-choice tests are used. Multiple-choice tests are more sensitive measures of available responses

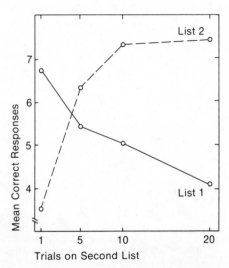

FIGURE 33   Free recall of both first- and second-list responses in an A-B, A-D design.

than free-recall tests. When multiple-choice tests are given immediately after second-list learning, almost 100 percent of the first-list responses are recognized (Postman & Stark, 1969). Individual responses from the second list do not replace corresponding responses to the same stimuli in the first list. Rather, there is general suppression of first-list responses that makes them difficult to recall even though they can be recognized on a multiple-choice test.

More generally, it is frequently true that the type of test that is given determines the degree of success that we achieve in remembering. When we are required to produce a verbal response, we may report that the answer is on the tip of our tongue but that we cannot quite speak it. It has been found that subjects could predict with better-than-chance accuracy which questions missed on a recall test they could remember on a multiple-choice test (Freedman & Landauer, 1966). Recall can be aided if the first letter of the response being sought is provided as a cue. Thus, our memories are fragmentary, composed of multiple components, and these may not be enough to produce a response in a recall test, but still be sufficient to judge the correct answer on a multiple-choice test.

Proactive Interference

Competition at the time of recall includes not only new responses learned since the original learning but also responses that were learned prior to testing of the learning. Figure 34 shows the effect of having several successive tests of short-term retention of nonsense syllables. Recall on

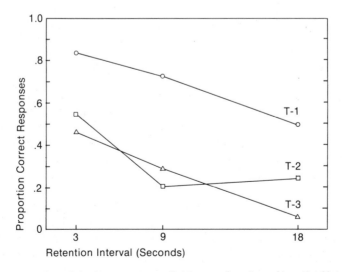

FIGURE 34   Retention of single consonant syllables as a function of length of interval and number of prior syllables.

the first test of the session for a subject was quite good, but on the second test recall occurred less frequently, and with the third test there was somewhat more forgetting (Keppel & Underwood, 1962). Erroneous letters recalled tended to come from recent items, as can be seen in Figure 35. On the sixth test of a short-term retention experiment in which three-letter messages were presented, the errors were found to be related to the recency with which the erroneous letter had been presented (Peterson & James, 1967). Memory for the letters in the current message is subject to competition from letters in previous messages.

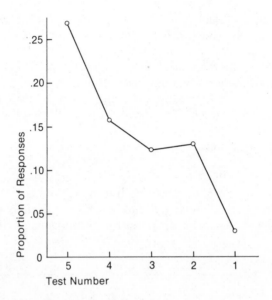

FIGURE 35   Source of intrusions on the sixth test.

Proactive interference can be dramatically reduced by a technique devised by Wickens (1972). Three successive tests of three-element messages are given to subjects, and then for the fourth message some characteristic is changed. For instance, in one condition the first three messages each consisted of three words, while the fourth message was made up of three spelled numbers (Wickens, 1972). Recall on the fourth test was greatly improved over the third test (see Figure 36). The improvement was due to change in type of message, for subjects switching from numbers to words also improved. The type of item that was presented furnished a cue which reduced competition from other items.

Other characteristics can be changed to reduce proactive interference, as by shifting from auditory to visual presentation. Categorical features might be changed, as in shifting from names of articles of furniture in one

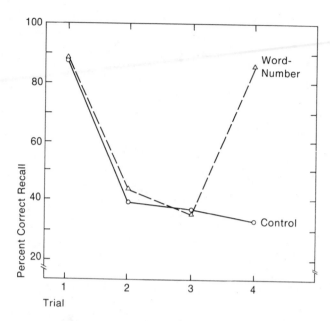

FIGURE 36   Illustration of reducing practice interference by shifting between the classes of spelled-out numbers and common words.

test to varieties of food in the next. Or, background relationships might be changed, as in shifting from white numerals against a black background to black numerals against a white background. In general, changes in contextual characteristics as well as in class of elements produce improved recall after the shift.

In addition to producing forgetting in short-term retention, proactive interference influences memory for lists of verbal items over long intervals of time. Underwood (1957) has shown that recall of a list after a 24-hour retention interval is markedly reduced by having learned previous lists. It is as if we learn to forget, since the more lists that have been learned, the poorer is the recall of the last one. In Figure 37 it can be seen that when no previous lists were learned, recall of a single list after 24 hours was about 75 percent correct. When five previous lists had been memorized, recall was only 25 percent correct. Earlier learning competed with the most recent learning, and this competition produced forgetting.

Organization of material during original learning has a considerable effect on sensitivity of the learning to interference. Dramatic improvement in recall results from instructions to organize subject matter. In one study (Bower & Clark, 1969) a group of subjects was told to make up a story linking a list of words together, while the control group was simply told to memorize the list. In both groups, a series of twelve lists was learned, one list after the other. Recall of a list was almost 100 percent correct for both

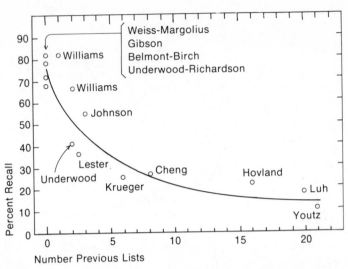

FIGURE 37   Recall as a function of number of previous lists as measured in a number of studies.

groups of subjects immediately after a list had been learned. However, when recall of all lists was tested at the end of the session, large differences appeared. The subjects who had devised stories remembered 93 percent of the words, while the other group recalled only 15 percent. The organized lists were resistant to interference from competing lists, whereas the unorganized lists were highly susceptible to combined proactive and retroactive interference.

Decay Versus Interference

Even though interference from other behavioral events is the major factor in forgetting, one may ask whether there may not be some forgetting when no other behavioral events either intervene during a retention interval or precede learning so as to produce proactive interference. Such an isolated event is not easy to examine experimentally; it is difficult to imagine. Even during sleep there is behavioral activity in the form of movements and speech, and forgetting does occur though less than during waking activity. Nevertheless, there are experimental situations which suggest to some psychologists that spontaneous decay of memory at the physiological level does occur. One such experiment (Posner, 1964) examined retention after differing rates of presentation of the message. From the point of view of a decay interpretation, retention should be better with a fast rate of presentation than with a slow rate of presentation since less time elapses from beginning of the message to the time of recall.

Of course, another variable—rehearsal—works in the opposite direction, since there is more time for rehearsal with a slow rate of presentation, and this should improve retention. In spite of rehearsal working against the effect of decay, fast rates of presentation have resulted in better recall than slow rates, at least in some experiments.

A recent study (Hockey, 1973) indicates that the effect of varying rate of presentation depends on what the subject does during learning. Sequences of digits of uncertain length (16–35) were presented, and subjects were instructed to recall as many of the last of a sequence as possible, a task known as a test of running memory. One group of subjects was instructed to be active in rehearsing and grouping digits by threes, while another group was told to avoid any organization of the digits and listen passively. The two kinds of instruction produced opposite trends in relation to rate of presentation (see Figure 38). Active rehearsal resulted in better recall the slower the rate of presentation, while passive listening produced poorer recall the slower the rate. The improvement with more time for active rehearsal is readily understood; the deterioration of recall for the passive group at slower rates of presentation suggests forgetting due to factors other than interference from behavioral events.

Evidence against decay interpretations is seen in experiments which show little forgetting over an interval of time. In a follow-up to the study graphed in Figure 34 in which a brief auditory presentation was used, Keppel and Underwood (1962) gave subjects a two-second visual exposure to three letters. Subjects showed virtually 100 percent correct recall of the letters on the initial test of the session. With this greater opportunity to learn the message, an interval of eighteen seconds filled

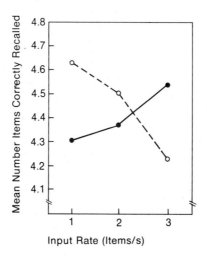

FIGURE 38   Total recall as a function of input rate and strategy.

with counting did not produce forgetting. Even though decay could not produce forgetting in this set of conditions, proactive interference could produce forgetting, as subsequent tests in the session showed. Of course, after the auditory presentations of Figure 34 there was forgetting on the first test, so it could be argued that decay can produce forgetting when the initial learning is not at a high level.

A striking failure to find forgetting found five unrelated letters recalled after an interval of 40 seconds with an accuracy better than 90 percent (Shiffrin, 1973). The task occupying the subject during the retention interval was the critical factor, since with performance of arithmetic during the interval forgetting was substantial. Little forgetting occurred when the distracting activity was a nonverbal task requiring the subject to detect a tone sounding faintly in a background of noise. Similar results were obtained when the messages were three words (Reitman, 1971). In this case significant forgetting was found when the subject listened for a speech sound against a background of noise composed of a different speech sound. Even such a minor use of verbal mechanisms by the subject produces some forgetting.

The failure to find forgetting over an interval filled with detection of tones is of interest only if the subject has not rehearsed during the interval. Subjects report that they have not rehearsed, and in the study by Shiffrin they were rewarded only for their performance on the detection task, not the memory task. Furthermore, if the distracting task is changed to arithmetic so that substantial forgetting occurs, a period of detection of tones prior to the interval of arithmetic does not reliably improve retention. Since rehearsal does improve retention, failure to find improvement after an interval filled with detection suggests that rehearsal is effectively minimized during motivated detection of tones.

The conclusion to which the evidence points is that interference in one form or another is the major factor in forgetting. There is a massive amount of evidence which demonstrates interference produces forgetting, and any role for decay of memories due to nonbehavioral events is a minor one.

7

Skilled Performance

Learning to perform skillfully involves more than motor learning. Responses must be coordinated with external stimuli, and it is appropriate to call the acquisition of skill, perceptual-motor learning. In learning to play tennis one not only has to know how to hold the racket and how to swing the arm to meet the ball squarely, one must learn to adjust these motor responses to deal with balls coming from different angles and traveling at various speeds.

Much skilled performance involves complex response systems made of simple components. The coordination of a sequence of parts into a smooth whole requires lengthy practice, and the acquisition of skill in a complex task extends over long periods of time beyond the elimination of gross errors. Responses are not simply right or wrong, as was the case in many of the tasks discussed in earlier chapters, but often there are gradations of response, making possible measured amounts of error in skilled performance.

STAGES IN ACQUISITION OF SKILL

Early Stage

Fitts (1964) has identified three stages of skill learning on the basis of laboratory observations and interviews with instructors. The requirements of any task are likely to be different as the learner progresses, and the expert doesn't face quite the same task as the beginner.

The early stage may be of short duration for the adult because of transfer from previous learning. Very little is completely new for the human adult, and the individual parts of a new task usually involve some familiar components. Of course, some aspects of past learning may have a negative influence.

In the early stage of skill learning, the parts of the task are small tasks in themselves, and instructions by an expert are beneficial in identifying the components. Demonstrations are likewise helpful, and the individual can learn much by observation. Active participation may be more useful than observation, and imagined practice also can result in improvement. For example, Ulich (1967) found imagined practice to be more beneficial than observation in a simple task requiring three sticks to be inserted in one of several holes. Imagined practice may even be more effective than actual practice in learning to keep a pointer on target (Rawlings, Rawlings, Chase, & Yilk, 1972).

Initially the learner attends to cues that may not be needed later. The inexperienced automobile driver looks for the pedals, and the beginning dancer looks at his feet. The learner has to attend to various parts of his body in order to relate them to objects in the environment. Typists may find it helpful to see what their fingers are doing in initial sessions, but visual cues will later be replaced by tactile and kinesthetic cues.

The task in the early stage is a collection of individual habits, and it bears a superficial resemblance to the skill that will develop after long practice. The change in emphasis on various components of the task is shown in Figure 39. Fleishman and Hempel (1954) used the techniques of factor analysis to identify the contribution of various components of a task to successive stages of learning. Note how rate of movement is relatively unimportant initially, while it assumes greater weight in later stages of practice. Visualization, on the other hand, is more important at first than later on. The graph was based on a complex perceptual-motor task studied with a battery of tests which measured the specific component factors portrayed in the figure.

A chief source of difficulty in the early stage is a failure to understand what has to be learned. Ingenious instructors have devised many ways to aid understanding through the use of verbal instructions, charts, and diagrams. Occasionally a model may provide simplified three-dimensional embodiment of the relationships underlying a task. An intriguing illustration is found in studies of the mending of woolen cloth so that the tear is invisible (Belbin, Belbin, & Hill, 1957). The difficulty of this task lies in acquiring a sequence of "unders and overs" related to the underlying structure of the weaves. The problem of comprehension was solved by having learners make elastic weaves on frames, followed by the use of mending cloth of extra large weave. This training transferred to cloth with weave of a standard size, markedly decreasing the length of time required to learn the task.

Intermediate Stage

Once the succession of individual components has been identified so that the learner knows the contents of each one, continued practice

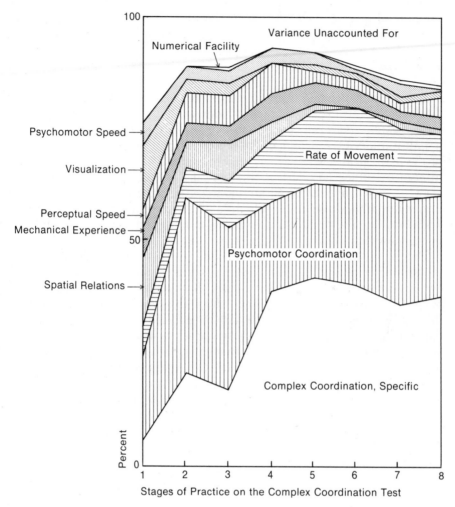

FIGURE 39   Components of skill in successive stages of learning.

eliminates errors. Errors include getting a component out of order, attending to the wrong cue, or inserting an extraneous component.

The intermediate stage may last for hours, or it may last for days, depending on the complexity of the task. In the case of learning the Morse code, the bulk of the errors are eliminated in the first ten hours of practice. In a very different kind of task, pilot training, serious errors are sufficiently reduced after about ten hours of instruction so that the student may be permitted to solo. In contrast to these examples, less time is required for subjects to stop making errors in a paired-associate learning task. The time required to eliminate errors during the intermediate portions of most skill learning is great enough so that it is usually spread over several days, rather than being accomplished in a single session.

Late Stage

When errors on a task cease, there still is room for improvement. In the late stage of learning a skill, the components of the task become routine to a large extent. Performers work more or less automatically, not having to attend to individual details of the performance. They can carry on much of the activity at the same time that they think about something else or even do another task. The piano player can continue playing while carrying on a conversation without missing a beat; the average automobile driver can drive down the street while listening to the news on the radio. These skills have become autonomous and are performed automatically in routine situations.

The extent to which a task can become automatic depends in part on relationships among changing external stimuli. The less predictable environmental stimuli are, the greater the demands of the task on the subject and the less attention left over for another task. This can be seen in the study by Bahrick and Shelly (1958) graphed in Figure 40. A serial reaction task with four lights was practiced for twenty-five days over a six-week period. Subjects were instructed to use their right hands to press one of four keys corresponding to one of the lights as soon as the light went on for a brief moment. A hit was scored if the key was pressed while the light was still on, and the task was learned to nearly 100 percent accuracy by the second day's session. The data of interest are those on Sessions 3, 14, and 25, when an auditory task was introduced which required responding with the other (left) hand at the same time that the visual task continued. The graph in Figure 40 depicts performance on the visual task for all sessions. On the days when the auditory task was performed concurrently with the visual task, performance was related to how predictable the sequences of stimuli were. In a *repetition* condition (RP), a stereotyped pattern of four lights was repeated over and over. In the completely random sequence (RA), each light and each combination of two lights in a row appeared equally often in an unpredictable order. Two other conditions were arranged between these two extremes. On the sessions in which two tasks were performed, the more uncertain the stimulus sequence, the poorer the performance on the visual task. There was improvement on the concurrent visual task on Session 14 as compared with Session 3, but thereafter no improvement was observed.

An automatic performance is clearly related to dependence of the response on external stimulation. In the limiting case where performance is independent of changing stimulation, as when a response sequence of the repetitive type does not have to be coordinated with external stimulation, performance of one concurrent task should be little impaired

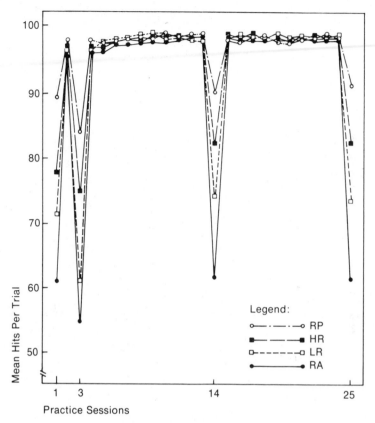

FIGURE 40   Performance on a visual task. During Sessions 3, 14, and 25 an auditory task was performed concurrently, while only the visual task was performed in other sessions.

by another task. For example, counting or alphabetizing rapidly aloud permits efficient concurrent performance of other tasks such as solving anagrams or adding digits (Peterson, 1969).

Limit

It may seem that improvement in any skill must eventually slow, so that there is a limit to what practice can accomplish. However, such a limit is reached less frequently than might be supposed. Sometimes a limit is set by the requirements of a machine that is being operated, so the limit can be readily determined. This is true of cigar-making, a skill of practical importance for some persons (Crossman, 1959). Figure 41 shows the time it takes to make cigars on a manually operated device as a function of time on the job. The study observed machine operators with differing amounts of experience. The rate at which the operators produced cigars was higher

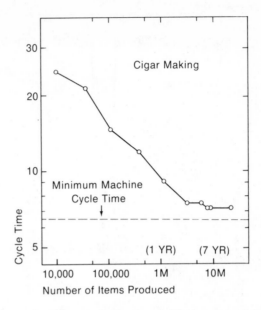

FIGURE 41   Rate of cigar making by operators of differing amounts of experience.

the greater their experience, so that eventually they approached a limit set by the time that it takes the machine to work.

Skills do not necessarily improve with practice. Motivation is required, or the learner may not stick with the job long enough to make long-term improvement possible. Even if he continues practicing, the poorly motivated learner may stop improving at a level far below that which could be attained with higher motivation.

There are few laboratory studies which have been carried out for long periods of time, since studies are usually terminated early for the convenience of all concerned. The study of cigar-making was a field study in which different workers provided the various amounts of experience. One of the longer laboratory studies on humans was carried out by Snoddy (1926) over a period of sixty days. Subjects learned to trace a pattern with a pencil when the sight of the hand was reversed in a mirror; one trial a day was given on the mirror-drawing. The results are shown in Figure 42. A combination of time and number of errors was recorded. Performance improved throughout the experiment, although the rate of improvement slowed toward the end. The logarithm of the measure of performance is shown plotted against the logarithm of the trial number. Without this transformation of the data, the performance would change more slowly, but there is no indication that improvement stopped at the end of the experiment.

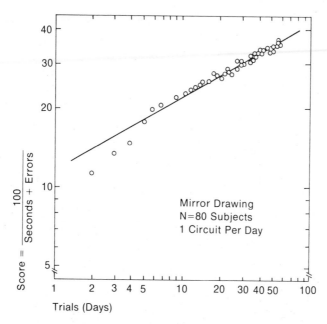

FIGURE 42   Extended practice on mirror-drawing.

The finding that improvement slows as practice continues for a few hours has sometimes led investigators to think that learning was leveling off after an initial burst. Practical considerations of limited time and money motivated the experimenters, and with longer practice other conclusions might have been reached. Skills learned outside the laboratory may continue to improve for years. Sometimes it is difficult to distinguish between the improvement due to maturation of the body and improvement resulting from practice, but various skills improve over several years. Often it is not feasible to observe the same individual for extended periods, but sampling of different individuals at various age levels can afford some illustration of improvement in skill learning.

Kay (1969) studied films of two-year-olds, five-year-olds, and fifteen-year-olds as they attempted to catch a ball that was tossed toward them. He reported that the two-year-olds held the palms together without immediately closing the fingers after the ball hit the hands. The hands moved together slowly, cradling the ball against the body, and of course the ball often rolled away. The children watched their hands or the thrower instead of following the ball with their eyes. In comparison, the five-year-old children moved their hands to meet the ball when it fell short and watched the ball in flight as well as their hands. The fifteen-year-olds kept their eyes on the ball even though they were moving their hands to the point of anticipated contact. Their hands closed quickly on the ball, and the whole performance was smooth and well coordinated. Kay noted that the five-year-old child was beginning to approach adult performance.

Other examples of lengthy periods of improvement are found among athletes who practice diligently year after year before reaching a peak. Top-notch musicians work many years to perfect their skills, and even the most proficient must continue to practice to keep their skill from deteriorating. For most persons there are few skills in which they have reached the limit of their potential.

THE ROLE OF FEEDBACK

The concept of feedback has some similarity to the concept of reinforcement. Both refer to stimulation which follows a response, but simple transfer of the reinforcement principle based on operant conditioning to learning a complex motor task may not have a predictable effect. Kahneman and Tversky (1973) have described the case of flight instructors who attempted to use positive reinforcement whenever a student executed a maneuver in a better than average manner. The instructors became convinced that positive reinforcement brought poorer performance, because every time they reinforced a student, the student did poorer on the next maneuver. The problem was that in a complex motor coordination performance can vary widely from one time to the next depending on chance factors, so that an unusually good performance was apt to be followed by an average one.

The concept of feedback resembles reinforcement in that it provides information. It informs the student how close a response was to the standard, not simply that his response was good or bad. By providing information, feedback enables the performer to adjust his response to more closely approach the target. In general, there are two kinds of feedback: *intrinsic* feedback provided by the performer's own movement, and *augmented* feedback from an instructor or some mechanical device which amplifies some aspect of performance.

Intrinsic Feedback

Movement of limbs of the body provides visual, tactual, and kinesthetic feedback to the performer. Playing a piano permits the player to see what the hands are doing, feel the hands pressing against the keys, and most importantly hear the sounds produced. As the player becomes expert, there is less dependence on the visual sense, and feedback from other senses plays a greater role.

The violin player illustrates continued graded adjustment of motor performance to feedback from responses. As the violinist hears a tone, the finger pressing against the string can be quickly moved just enough to correct the pitch of the sound. The adjustment can continue until a tone is heard which matches the internal standard which defines for the performer what the tone should be.

Feedback is conceived as an essential part of a closed loop which permits constant correction of errors and fine adjustment of responses. A diagram illustrating a closed loop analysis of motor learning and performance is shown in Figure 43 (Chase, 1965). Stimuli from the environment are processed in the organism's nervous system, and the response to the stimulation produces feedback into the sensory systems which then is processed along with new environmental stimulation. There is continuous responding, feedback, and correction of error in a closed loop.

Reducing feedback can result in deteriorating performance in many tasks, but some learning without feedback is possible. In a simple key-tapping task with kinesthetic and tactual feedback minimized by a pressure cuff on the arm together with a blindfold eliminating visual cues and earphones minimizing auditory cues, subjects can still improve tapping performance (Lazlo, 1967). Subjects report that the pressure cuff eliminates all sensation in the hand after an initial tingling sensation. In spite of apparent absence of sensory feedback, movements can be made and tapping improved to within 79 percent of normal tapping speed in eight 40-second training sessions. Of course, reduction of feedback impaired performance initially, and training was necessary to get anything approaching adequate performance.

There are tasks in which improvement is not possible without feedback. The same comprehensive reduction in feedback described above was applied to the task of drawing letters with the index finger (Lazlo & Bairstow, 1971). The drawing could not be done efficiently, and no improvement with practice could be measured. The fine motor control required for such a task as tracing a letter required some minimal sensory feedback.

Augmented Feedback

In many situations the intrinsic feedback is slight, and the acquisition of skill difficult. Interpretation of the intrinsic feedback from movements of the body has to be learned, and prominent visual cues ignored. In cases of this kind, augmented feedback may assist the learner temporarily. An instructor may advise students what they are doing wrong, or some mechanical device may be used to amplify subtle cues that are difficult for beginners to detect. The objective is to discontinue the augmented feedback after the intrinsic cues can be discriminated adequately.

The value of augmented feedback depends on maintenance of natural sources of stimulation after the augmented feedback has been withdrawn. This was illustrated in a study (Adams, Goetz, & Marshall, 1972) of arm positioning, a ten-inch displacement of the arm accompanying the

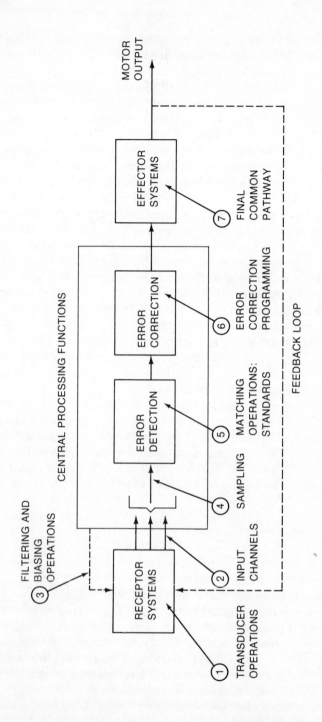

FIGURE 43   Flow diagram of a system for the control of motor activity.

movement of a slide along a track. Subjects were not informed of the length of the required movement, and they received knowledge of results after each response by announcement of the direction and amount of error in eighths of an inch. After this series of acquisition trials, knowledge of results was discontinued, so there was no longer any feedback from the experimenter. Different groups of subjects received differing amounts of visual, auditory, and kinesthetic feedback from their own movements during acquisition. Some could see their movements, hear the sound of the slide, and feel the tension from pulling the slide against the spring that held it in place. Other subjects wore goggles, heard irrelevant noise over earphones, and had no tension on the slide. As might be expected, subjects were more accurate in their movements with maximal feedback both during acquisition and after withdrawal of knowledge of results. Of greater interest was the finding that performance after withdrawal of knowledge of results was poorest when visual and kinesthetic feedback conditions were changed from acquisition to withdrawal. For instance, for subjects with minimal feedback, error after withdrawal was less when there also had been minimal feedback during acquisition. Subjects with minimal feedback learned during acquisition to use what cues were available. When these minimal cues were changed, even though stimulation was intensified, subjects could not interpret these cues very well.

CENTRAL FACTORS

It is sometimes assumed that motor learning can be readily analyzed in terms of a stimulus-response chaining model. Stimuli produce appropriate responses which in turn produce feedback which is added to the new stimulus input. However, processes in the central nervous system play an important role. For instance, improvement in performance on one limb can follow practice with the other limb, a phenomenon known as *bilateral transfer.* Learning to tap rapidly with the index finger under conditions of minimal feedback improves tapping on the unpracticed hand (Lazlo & Baguley, 1971). Since different muscles in the two hands are involved, the learning must involve something other than the peripheral muscles and their immediately associated neurons.

Internal Standards

One central factor in motor performance is the development of an internal perceptual standard against which feedback from performance can be compared. For example, one has to know what music should sound like in order to play well. One approach to teaching children to play stringed instruments emphasizes listening to music of good quality before attempting to produce music. The Suzuki method, which originated in Japan, requires parents to play recorded music for their children shortly after birth, playing the same number over and over again until it becomes very familiar (Pronko, 1969). Only after several pieces of music have become familiar is the child of three or four years given a violin and permitted to play. By this time he has an internal standard against which he can compare the sounds he makes.

Memory for sensory experiences in various sensory modes can become the basis for internal standards. Visual imagery based on past experience is more significant for many individuals than auditory imagery, and spatial relationships learned and stored in the past assist our movements through space. Fixing a map in memory before entering new territory is a preparation adopted by prudent travelers. One who has lived in a house for some time will be able to move about even when the storm knocks out the lights, although such a person may not do as well as the blind person who has had to more fully develop internal maps.

Motor Programs

Another central factor involves motor programs which can control movement in the absence of feedback. Since one can perform gross movements, at the least, in the absence of clear feedback, there must be central programs which can carry out a series of movements without guidance from sensory feedback (Lazlo, 1967). Such movements cannot be corrected, but the general outline of a series of movements can be carried out in the proper order. In normal performance, the motor program makes fine adjustments in response to feedback (Keele, 1973).

The coordination of a motor program with feedback from its use was seen in a study of tracking a spot of light on an oscilloscope (Pew, 1966). The task was to keep the spot of light as near the center of the screen as possible by pressing one or the other of two keys. On depressing the left key the spot accelerated to the left, while pressing the right key accelerated the spot to the right. Since the spot had rapid movement of its own, it could be kept in the center of the screen only by rapidly pressing first one key and then the other. Analysis of response patterns indicated that some subjects adopted the plan of alternating very rapidly between the keys, without waiting for individual movements off target before making a compensating key press. On this semiautomatic alternation, subjects imposed a tendency to linger a little longer on one key rather than the other in order to correct for a drift off target. The rapid alternation, without regard to consequence, can be interpreted as the result of a motor program; in addition, the motor program is modified to adjust the timing to the drift off target. In a sense subjects apply a basic drum beat to their performances not unlike that of a musical performance, but depending on the visual feedback of the moment they change the accent or stress in the continuing rhythm.

Organization

Perceptual-motor learning is not just a matter of connecting a set of stimuli to a set of responses randomly paired with the stimuli. If some organized relationships linking stimuli and responses can be perceived, learning will proceed more rapidly. The stimulus-response *compatibility* of the learning task is a significant factor in difficulty of the learning.

For example, if there are four lights in a stimulus display, and each light has a key beneath it which is supposed to be pressed when the light flashes on, the arrangement has a high degree of compatibility. On the other hand, if the keys are randomly assigned to the lights, so that when the leftmost light flashes the third key from the left must be pressed, then there is low compatibility between stimulus and response. The more compatible the assignment of stimuli to responses the easier the task will be to learn. If a pointer moves in the same direction as the wheel that the performer turns, then learning is faster than if the wheel goes in one direction and the pointer goes in the opposite direction. Compatibility is related to the associative component of perceptual-motor learning. Like verbal learning, perceptual-motor learning also involves relating stimuli to one another, integrating responses into unitary chunks, and associating stimuli with responses.

Many tasks are strongly influenced by *hierarchical organization*. A man in a workshop running a lathe is performing a series of acts which are highly structured (Welford, 1968). At the lowest level of organization, particular muscle actions are combined into a series, say twisting the wrist to turn a wheel. This act is one of a series required to machine one individual part, and the article being made might require a number of separate parts. The finished article, in turn, would be one of several needed for the complete order. Thus, there are units or chunks which combine to form higher-level chunks in a hierarchical organization.

The acquisition of a hierarchical organization has been studied in a simple perceptual-motor task (Restle & Brown, 1970). Six white lights with a red button beneath each light confronted the subject, and the task consisted of pressing buttons in the correct serial order in anticipation of the next light. The subjects were told there would be repeating patterns, but they did not know the nature of the patterns. The difficulty of different parts of a sequence were related to the organizational characteristics of a given sequence. Subjects discovered chunks such as "runs" and "trills." Runs were two or more adjacent lights occurring in succession, as when Lights 1, 2, and 3 came on successively. Trills consisted of repetitions of a short run, as in the succession 1, 2, 1, 2. Hence a trill is a higher order unit than a run.

Most errors occurred at the beginning of a new unit and decreased within the unit as in the example in Figure 44. Errors were greatest at the beginning of the highest level unit and lowest at beginnings of the lowest

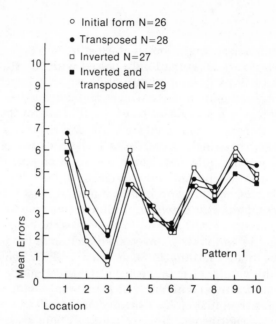

FIGURE 44   Error profile for variations of a light pattern of the following prototype: 1, 2, 3, 5, 4, 3, 3, 2, 3, 4. The pattern seems to have been organized into four groups as follows: (1, 2, 3) (5, 4, 3) (3, 2) (3, 4). Errors were most numerous at the beginning of each group.

level units. For instance, the pattern 1, 2, 1, 2, 6, 5, 6, 5 could be analyzed into four runs of two lights, at the lowest level of organization. At a higher level, there are two groups of two runs each making up two trills, the second trill being a mirror image of the first. The most difficult point was at the beginning of the second trill, at the highest level of organization. The transition from the first to the second element in a run was the easiest to learn.

Structured sequences like these are easier to learn than nonstructured sequences, and pretraining subjects on samples of runs and trills assist later performance. These experiments also indicate that hierarchical organization is not limited to verbal learning.

CONDITIONS OF PRACTICE

Factors discussed in previous sections have implications for optimum conditions for acquisition of skills. Feedback can be augmented to speed acquisition; the task can be organized to provide rapid progress. In addition to these and other practical implications already discussed, there are two factors—distribution of practice and part versus whole learning—which have been the object of considerable research in the search for optimum conditions of practice.

Distribution of Practice

A practical problem of some importance in skill learning concerns the arrangement of rest intervals during practice. Is it better to try to compress practice into as few periods as possible, with as little time lost between periods as is feasible, or is it advantageous to introduce frequent rest periods?

In general, practice distributed over substantial periods of time produces better performance than massed practice. However, the type of task to be learned should be considered. For example, a task with a substantial memory requirement may suffer if too long a period elapses between trials. On the other hand, repetition of a task without rest periods might produce a bored and fatigued subject.

Figure 45 depicts the results of a pursuit-rotor experiment (Bourne & Archer, 1956) in which subjects learned to keep a pointer fixed on a spot on a revolving disc. After examining a number of different rest intervals, it was found that the longer the rest period the greater the percent of time spent on target. There was a particularly large improvement after the five-minute rest interval, as shown by the break in the curve.

The need for rest intervals is not produced by muscle fatigue alone. Consider a study of vigilance in which the subject waited to detect a signal which didn't occur very often. No great muscle effort was required, but the subject had to be ready at all times to detect a possible signal. Even highly trained subjects showed poor performance when there were no rest

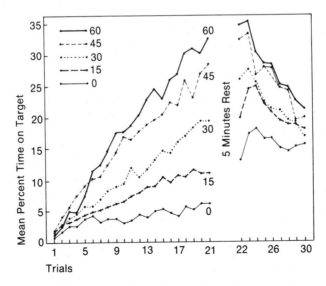

FIGURE 45   Time on target as a function of distribution of practice. Subjects had intervals of 0 to 60 seconds between trials.

intervals over long periods of time (Mackworth, 1964). In this case inactivity of the muscles did not mean rest in a psychological sense.

Part Versus Whole

Should a complex skill be practiced in parts or as a whole? Should the beginning swimmer practice arm strokes separately from the kick? There are no rigid rules, but in general with a difficult skill, the beginner needs to study one thing at a time. He has to learn what is involved in some crude way. When the skill involves the performance of several independent actions concurrently, practice of the parts may be advantageous. However, when synchronization of the parts is necessary for the task, the major aspect of the learning may involve the timing of individual components. Under these circumstances the sooner the skill can be performed as a whole, the better will be the results.

A compromise technique is the *progressive-part* method (Welford, 1968). Individual parts are practiced initially. Then a few are practiced together, and further components are added gradually, so that the number of additional task components at any one time is small. Each new combination is learned relatively quickly and thoroughly, and the overall task is efficiently mastered. This technique works in such disparate tasks as lathe operation and the sorting of mail, as well as in learning lists of nonsense syllables.

8

Thinking

Thinking is not independent from the processes already discussed, for the organism that thinks is the same one that is conditioned, memorizes words, and develops skills. Thinking itself can be considered a skill which utilizes past learning and present perceptions.

What is distinctive about thinking? Thinking differs from other behavior in that it involves representational activity which substitutes for actual movements through space. Naturally, looking into the future requires recalling similar past situations; however, when we think, we acquire independence from the restrictions of time and place. In thought we can view the world, not just as it is, or was, but as it could be. Thinking is goal oriented, directed at solving problems or winning games. The product of thought may be new only to the individual or it may be novel in human history.

Thinking will be analyzed first in terms of underlying representations and conceptual structures. Then, the utilization of these structures in solving problems and playing games will be considered.

REPRESENTATION

Animal Representation

The use of symbols is not confined to humans. Hull considered the fractional anticipatory response a primitive type of symbol. Recent work with chimpanzees has demonstrated the ability of that animal to use gestures to represent many objects and actions (Gardner & Gardner, 1969). The chimp can learn some of the signs used by deaf humans. However, it is not adept at making sounds that resemble speech, and the number of vocal sounds that it can reproduce is limited.

Premack (1971) has taught a chimpanzee the rudiments of language behavior through the use of visual symbols. Words are represented by pieces of plastic varying in color, size, and shape, and each word has a metal back so that it will stick to a magnetic board. The chimp, Sarah, can compose a sentence by placing words one above the other, or answer a question by completing a sentence.

Among the questions which Sarah can answer are those involving classification of labels for objects. The words for banana, grape, and peach are classified together as fruit. Cracker, cookie, and bread are classified as "not-fruit."

Sarah has learned names for properties or attributes of objects. She knows a word for color and a word for shape. After being taught to use red and yellow accurately, she could answer a question relating red to apple by use of the plastic block for color. After learning round and square, she could apply these accurately in response to questions.

Premack used instrumental conditioning techniques in training Sarah. She was reinforced with food for making responses such as picking up a word and placing it on the magnetic board. The relatively sophisticated language behavior that Sarah acquired grew out of an accumulation of discriminations learned over a period of time. Not stopping with learning labels for objects, she learned labels for attributes of objects as well as labels for classes of attributes. This is appropriately called concept learning.

Human Representation

Humans, like lower animals, can represent objects and events by gestures. The deaf use fairly elaborate systems of signs to communicate. The public speaker makes some use of gestures, although they are not as precise as the sign language of the deaf. The earliest representational efforts of the infant involve the use of *action,* as in the shaking movement that represents an absent rattle (Bruner, 1964).

Humans make considerable use of images to represent objects. Representation in visual forms can take on varying degrees of abstractness: Humans can be represented by stick figures; the countryside need not look like the map that aims to represent it. Visual representation begins early in the child and continues to a greater or lesser degree into adult life.

Verbal symbols eventually become a major factor in the thinking of children. In addition to learning labels for objects and attributes, they learn abstract verbal terms which represent complex concepts embedded in networks of interrelated verbal symbols. Mathematics is one such abstract system; language is another. Specific subject areas have their own systems of concepts, and the child's thinking in each area will be dominated by the corresponding terms that he has acquired.

The advantages of being able to use language are great. Recording it by various means permits permanent storage in compact form. Verbal representations also can be stored internally to be produced later in the absence of the objects and events to which they refer.

CONCEPT LEARNING

The child at an early age develops the capacity to classify events and objects in the world around him. Children as young as twelve months have been found to classify objects (Ricciuti, 1965). If four beads and four clay balls are spread haphazardly in front of a child, the child will respond to the suggestion to play with the objects. Children can sort out the beads from the other objects, either by touching them or by placing them together at one side. Such classificatory behavior precedes language development; it basically consists of the identification of relevant attributes.

Attribute Identification

One way of studying attribute identification is through discrimination-learning studies of the kind described in Chapter 4. A variety of attributes are present in the task, and the experimenter reinforces appropriate responses to the relevant attributes. The difficulty of discovering the relevant attributes depends on the number of irrelevant as well as relevant attributes that are present. In most such studies, the laboratory subjects are not learning a new concept, since they are familiar with the concepts of color, size, and shape that form the dimensions of variation of the stimuli. Rather they are using their conceptual knowledge to solve a problem which the experimenter has arranged. Many investigators have assumed that the process of identifying attributes in this transfer situation is also essential to learning new concepts.

There is evidence to support the view that the discovery of relevant attributes is the basis of concept learning. The evidence is found in studies of children who have yet to acquire some concept that is normally used by an adult. One such concept—that of the diagonal—is acquired by most children sometime between the ages of three and six. When children are shown a checkerboard with one row or column filled with checkers, children of three can duplicate on their own boards the row or column they have seen, but few will be able to reproduce a diagonal running from one corner to the opposite corner. As children grow older they are more likely to be able to duplicate a diagonal, but acquisition is slow if children are left to themselves. A simple demonstration and correction procedure does not seem to be helpful; children must be specifically directed to attend to the corners. Then, the line linking one corner to another through the middle must be noted. Simply giving names to the attributes is not enough; rather, the verbal instructions must lead children to make their own observations, to attend to the attributes (Olson, 1970).

Another difficult concept for young children is conservation of quantity (Bruner, 1967). Let a child of four watch you pour all the water from a tall, thin glass into a short, wide glass, and then ask the child if the amount of water in the second glass is the same as it was in the first glass. The four-year-old will usually say no. If you ask why, he may say that it was higher before. The child is misled by an irrelevant dimension.

Children who do not conserve may be trained to do so. Children of five have been given training to discriminate dimensions and quantities, when they were found not to conserve quantity. After learning many different problems, they were able to conserve on tests which they originally had failed (Gelman, 1969).

The study of eye movements provides some evidence as to what may be involved in failure to conserve (O'Bryan & Boersma, 1971). Eye movements of nonconservers had only a few fixations as they stared at the dominant visual features of the situation. On the other hand, conservers tended to make many fixations, as they scanned various features. In general many studies of training suggest that learning to attend to relevant cues is an essential part of forming concepts in everyday life, as it is a prominent part of concept-identification studies.

Rule Learning

In simple attribute identification, classification is based on values of one dimension of variation: Objects are classified on the basis of color, form, shape, or some other single dimension. Complex concepts may be classified on the basis of several dimensions. For example, both color and form may be relevant attributes, and a rule may link the two dimensions together.

Two-dimensional tasks can be studied by informing subjects which two attributes are relevant, and asking them to discover a rule relating the attributes. The rule might be *conjunction,* as when patterns that are both red and square would be instances of the concept. Or, the rule might be *disjunction,* so that patterns which were either red or square would be instances of the concept. A striking finding is that subjects learn how to discover rules.

Figure 46 summarizes an experiment (Bourne, 1970) in which twelve different problems were learned successively. Each block of three successive problems was based on the same type of rule—disjunction—but with different attributes involved. Subjects not only showed transfer from one problem to another as more problems on the same type of rule were given, but they showed improved learning of new rules. The results suggest that the subjects learned to fit individual rules together into a general conceptual system. As such, systems of classification as a general prob-

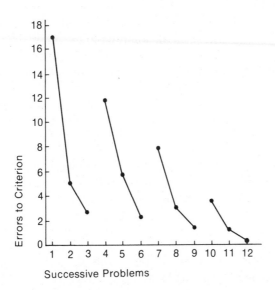

FIGURE 46   Learning to learn how to apply rules in attribute identification. Problems are blocked into sets of three, each block based on one of four rules.

lem-solving strategy were learned in addition to the individual rules. Individual stimuli were classified into four general classes, a classification scheme which permitted rapid acquisition of appropriate responses in new tasks.

Children learn conceptual systems not only in school but also in the home and at play. The discussion of semantic memory in Chapter 6 provided an example of a conceptual system of language concepts. Children learn labels for classes of objects and classes of attributes, and they also learn rules relating simple concepts to one another. The conceptual systems that adults have learned are not collections of independent concepts; rather, the conceptual systems are like networks of interconnected concepts.

In addition to systems of natural language concepts, children learn mathematical concepts which are related to one another by various rules, and which permit the precise solution of quantitative problems. For the majority of individuals these and other networks may be rudimentary and incomplete when compared to those of expert mathematicians. Nevertheless they function to influence our thinking to a greater or lesser degree, depending on how highly developed they are.

PROBLEM SOLVING

When one has learned ways of representing objects and events, and when conceptual systems have been acquired, these structures can be applied to the solution of problems. A problem can be viewed as a discrepancy between an initial situation and some desired situation, with solution consisting of discovery of a way to bridge the gap between the two (Greeno, 1973). Problems can be classified into static or *fixed problems* and *interactive problems*. Fixed problems depend only on the unopposed efforts of the solver, while interactive problems involve changing characteristics due to the actions of an opponent, as in playing a game.

Hypothesis Testing

Concept-identification experiments require solution of a fixed problem. Subjects are presented with sequences of stimuli which vary in attributes such as color, size, or shape, and the problem is to discover which attribute has been assigned to a particular response. Like other problem-solving tasks, concept identification can be viewed as a process of hypothesis testing. On a given trial, the subject samples one of a population of possible hypotheses and makes a response based on that hypothesis. The hypothesis is either confirmed or disconfirmed by knowledge of results supplied by the experimenter. If the hypothesis leads to an error, the subject tries another hypothesis.

If one assumes that hypotheses are sampled with replacement, so that the rejected hypothesis is put back into the pool to be resampled, a simple mathematical model can be applied (Restle, 1962). While a number of statistical measures derived from such a model seem to fit the process very well, one feature appears to be wrong. The subjects do not immediately test a hypothesis that has just been disconfirmed (Levine, 1962). On the other hand, the subject doesn't sample without replacement either, since hypotheses are sometimes tried again after a long interval.

Hypothesis testing has been measured directly by requiring subjects to press one of eight keys to obtain a visual display of some of the possible attributes (Millward & Spoehr, 1973). As many attributes as desired could be sampled on a given trial before making a classification response. In this way, by equating sampling of a hypothesis to pressing a key, information could be obtained about questions relating to sample size and replacement of eliminated hypotheses. In general, the average sample size before the trial of the last error was not found to vary significantly. However, after the last error, the size of the sample decreased systematically until after twelve problems the sample size was down to one hypothesis. In regard to replacement of hypotheses, subjects learned not to use eliminated hypotheses. Again this is clear evidence that assumptions of constant sample size and sampling with replacement are not justified by experimental data. Although a simple sampling model does not seem adequate, the general concept of hypothesis testing is useful. One approach is to conceive of the problem solver as moving on to a new class of hypotheses when an old set is exhausted (Levine, 1971). Whatever the specific details of the process may be, the subject, in solving a wide variety of problem-solving tasks, tests hypotheses.

Strategies

Strategies are broad approaches to solution of a problem and may determine the order in which hypotheses are tested in a given problem. The role of strategies in concept identification has been studied by permitting the subject to select possible instances of the concept, instead of having the subject passively observe instances presented by the experimenter (Bruner, Goodnow, & Austin, 1956). In the active selection experiment, the full population of stimulus instances was available throughout the experiment. Subjects had to choose cards which they thought might be instances of the concept. After each choice, subjects were told whether the choice was correct, and eventually they were able to identify the concept. Since subjects could choose the cards in any order, inferences were made about the way of proceeding. Subjects developed *strategies* to obtain information. Some subjects were efficient, while others proceeded with haphazard guessing. A number of strategies were observed in experiments with conjunctive concepts in which two or more different attributes had to be present in each positive instance of the concept.

A strategy of *conservative focusing* was the most efficient approach. With this strategy, the first hypothesis includes all attributes of the initial positive instance. As other instances are discovered, attributes which differ from the previous one can be eliminated, one at a time. For example, suppose that the first instance was a single red square with a line around the border. The initial hypothesis would include all four of those attributes. Suppose the subject then selects an instance which differs on one attribute, perhaps an instance with two red squares and a single line around the border. After being told that this also was a positive instance, the subject could reduce his hypothesis to "red square with one border line." Then, suppose he selects another instance with two black squares with a single border line, and is told this is also a positive instance. He can now reduce the hypothesis to "square with single border line."

The subject's first choice eliminated number as a dimension, while the second eliminated color. Of course, the stimulus instance he chose might not be a positive instance, but this would give him information, too, if one dimension is varied at a time. This is an efficient strategy, since it minimizes the memory requirements of the task. The subject need remember only a small number of chunks of information, and the number decreases as the experiment continues.

Conservative focusing can be distinguished from *focus gambling*. In the latter strategy, subjects change two or more attributes at a time, and if they are lucky, they may learn exceptionally fast. However, when a stimulus is chosen which is not an instance of the concept, a choice is wasted, since it is impossible to know which of the two changes was critical. On the average, focus gambling requires more trials to solution than conservative focusing.

Functional Fixedness

Some problem-solving tasks which initially do not seem to involve classification still require it. Consider a problem in which two strings hang from the ceiling, so far apart that a person cannot reach them both at the same time. The task is to tie the two strings together. The solution is to tie some object to one string and set it swinging like a pendulum. At the end of a swing, both strings can be grasped simultaneously.

In one version of this experiment, two heavy objects which could be used as a pendulum were provided, an electric switch and a relay (Birch & Rabinowitz, 1951). These objects were placed near the strings, but it was up to the subjects to choose one of them. The subjects were not familiar with these objects before the experiment, but they had used one of them in a preliminary wiring problem.

The solution of the problem took some time. Most subjects needed a hint, the hint being the experimenter brushing against one of the strings to set it swinging. All of the subjects solved the problem after the hint, but seventeen out of nineteen subjects used the object which had *not* been previously used in the wiring task as an electrical device. Once an object was classified as an electrical device, they did not think to use it as a weight, which is an example of *functional fixedness.*

The retention of functional fixedness also has been investigated (Adamson & Taylor, 1954). In a similar experiment, delays of various lengths were introduced between the wiring problem and the string problem. When a long interval separated the original experience from the test situation, the previous experience no longer influenced the solution of the problem.

Verbal labels have been found to be effective in calling attention to the critical element which the subject might otherwise overlook (Glucksberg & Weisberg, 1966). Subjects were instructed to attach a burning candle to the wall using only the objects set before them on a table. These objects included a candle, a booklet of matches, and a box filled with tacks. Subjects tended to overlook the possible use of the box as a shelf after emptying out the tacks. Wax from the candle could be used to fix the box to the wall. When the tacks were in the box, it was viewed as a container rather than a possible shelf, an instance of functional fixedness. This negative view was overcome by showing subjects a picture of the objects with labels pointing to each object, including separate labels for the box and the tacks. Subjects for whom the box was labeled solved the problem without difficulty.

Subgoals

Many complex problems can be broken down into components, with each subproblem being solved separately before achieving solution of the whole problem. The solution of each of the parts then constitutes a subgoal to be reached on the way to the major goal.

Subgoals have been studied experimentally in a spy problem in which subjects learned a list of links of communication between pairs of spies (Hayes, 1966). A typical list of connections is shown in Figure 47, which required paired-associate learning. The subject having learned the list was given a task in which he had to announce the steps involved in getting a message from Spy X to Spy Y; the names in the list each represented a spy's code name. There was a structure underlying the list that was learned, and this structure determined the difficulty of the task. The structure of the list is depicted in Figure 48. The time required for solution depended on the length of the true path, the number of blind alleys, and the length of the blind alleys. The time for announcing each step in the chain decreased as the subject neared the goal, and if subgoals were specified by the experimenter the time per step decreased as each subgoal was reached. Thus the experimenter might tell a subject to get a message through from shower to hill by way of larynx. Larynx then

```
SHOWER ──────► CLERK
DROUGHT ──────► HILL
LARYNX ──────► BETH
ADJECTIVE ──────► SHOWER
HILL ──────► HORSE
BEEF ──────► LARYNX
ADJECTIVE ──────► PARCHESI
DROUGHT ──────► KEVIN
SHOWER ──────► BEEF
LARYNX ──────► DROUGHT
BEEF ──────► TAFT
```

FIGURE 47   A typical list of spy connections.

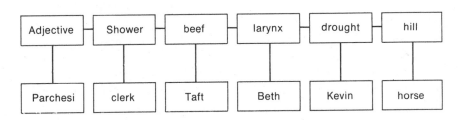

FIGURE 48   The structure underlying the list shown in Figure 47.

represented a subgoal, and the subject would speed up as this subgoal was approached and then slow down immediately after the subgoal was reached. In this case the experimenter had organized the problem for the subject in terms of subgoals.

Confronted with a complex problem, a problem solver engages in *means-ends analysis* (Newell & Simon, 1972). The problem is broken down into subproblems and even the subproblems into subproblems in some cases. For instance, the problem may be to obtain a college degree. This can be broken down into subproblems involving passing a set of courses in each of eight successive semesters. Each semester's work can be further analyzed into the component courses taken in each. The individual course can be further divided into successful passing of a certain number of tests. When the student reaches a subproblem of sufficiently small size, a possible solution for that subproblem may be recognized. Where a solution to a problem may seem hopeless, when subdivided into smaller parts the achievement of the subgoals may appear quite feasible. Transfer of hypotheses from other past solutions will occur even though the situations are not completely identical.

One advantage of thinking over the execution of a complex series of actions is that, through thought, the problem can be approached by starting at the goal and working backward. The thinker asks what the last step before achieving the goal would be. Having discovered that, the search continues for the step prior to that, and so on back to the present state of affairs. In the spy problem described earlier, subjects tended to use a backward strategy only after the forward strategy had failed. As a given individual continued to solve problems of different structure, the number of backward solutions increased until 35 to 40 percent of the problems were being solved with a backward strategy.

GAME PLAYING

Game playing can be viewed as an interactive form of problem solving. The problem solver interacts with one or more persons in a problem which changes from one play to the next. In contrast, problems such as concept identification, algebraic word problems, and other problems described earlier have constant components so that the demands on the solver are fixed. Game playing involves a succession of subproblems which are related to one another by having similar features from one play to the next and by having the common overall goal of achieving a winning position. The testing of hypotheses, the use of strategies, and means-ends analysis are all used in game playing as well as in fixed problems.

A board game such as chess requires the learning of a conceptual structure as a prerequisite to play. The names of various pieces must be learned, but more than involving just a label the concept of a specific piece involves knowing the kind of move that piece is permitted. A set of rules relates pieces to one another and to the goal of putting the opponent's king in check. Only after the rules are understood can the player begin to test hypotheses and form strategies for winning the game.

Planning Ahead

One aspect of game play that is not found in solving fixed problems is the anticipation of future moves by the opponent. It is not enough to consider the alternatives on a given move, but good players attempt to anticipate the opponent's response. The player sets up a plan several steps in advance based on judgment of the likely countermoves in response to one's own moves. The player's short-term memory limits the development of the plan, since the farther in advance thinking proceeds the greater the number of alternative paths will be possible. However, if both players are experts, responses to a given move can be highly predictable, and paths well into the future may be explored. The player can ignore obviously bad lines of play after scanning the initial possibilities, and instead concentrate on a particular chain of moves. *Progressive deepening* refers to broadening the analysis of the best move, exploring new alternatives farther ahead, and extending the planning for a longer series of moves (de Groot, 1965).

Dependence on memory in planning ahead raises the question of how the chess master achieves his skill. Does the master have an exceptional memory to begin with? No, code patterns of pieces and positions are learned, so that a familiar pattern becomes a chunk which can be recognized in a few seconds and stored as a unit (de Groot, 1966). The chess master is not superior to inferior players in memory for unorganized collections of details. Rather, chess masters are superior in recognizing arrangements which are familiar to them, since such patterns are likely ones in a game between expert players. Thinking depends on memory, which in turn hinges on perception of familiar patterns. Of course, the familiar pattern involves more than a spatial arrangement of pieces; it includes information such as a threat to the king that is only implicit in the visual features.

Learning to Play

The acquisition of skill in playing games is more easily studied in games that are simpler than chess. To become expert at chess requires years, while with a game such as gomoku several days may suffice to produce a master player. Therefore, it is more feasible for the psychologist with limitations on time to study the acquisition of skill in the simpler game.

Gomoku is played on an abbreviated checkerboard, 9 by 9 squares in size. Two players take turns placing one of their pieces on a vacant square, until one player gets five of his pieces in a row. The first player to accomplish this is the winner, whether the row is horizontal, vertical, or diagonal. Of course, the opponent tries to block the setting up of a row, and so shorter rows become important subgoals which may develop into winning positions.

The learning of gomoku has been studied in the laboratory by presenting the board on a television screen controlled by a computer (Kareev, 1973). The subject makes responses by touching a square on the screen with a pen to which the screen is sensitive. The player's opponent is the computer which has been programmed to play a good, but not an unbeatable game. Several special operations are available to the subject, including a preview technique and a look-back technique. In the preview mode, subjects can look ahead and see the consequences of possible moves without straining memory capacity. In the look-back mode, subjects can go back to an earlier position and note how they arrived at their present positions. These special modes were used only at the request of the subject, and one of the findings of the experiment was that subjects tended to ignore the look-back mode. They seemed to have little memory for previous steps. On the other hand they made considerable use of the preview mode, but this use depended on the nature of the previous move made by the computer. A move by the computer requiring immediate defensive reaction was not apt to be followed by use of the preview mode. In situations when the player was in greater doubt as to the next move that should be made, the preview was more likely to be used. Subjects were found to use primitive strategies even in the first game that they played, but they showed modest improvement as they continued to play.

Only a limited selection of problem-solving tasks has been mentioned, but from these it is clear that problem solving depends on the conceptual structures that the individual has acquired. The hypotheses that are tested in attempting to bridge the gap between the given situation and some objective are usually transferred from previous experience. Often the strategies used by the solver also are those used previously in similar situations. This transfer of hypotheses and strategies may benefit the solver or sometimes prove a hindrance. Usually one strategy that is a help is the breaking up of the problem into subproblems. Such a breakdown is forced on the problem solver in interactive tasks such as games.

9

Interpretations of Learning

Interpretations of learning process are products of thinking, and examining them will serve the dual purpose of furnishing illustrations of creative thinking and providing perspectives on possible integrations of various learning tasks. The result of an attempt to set forth systematic principles of a set of phenomena is called a theory. Theories are the result of creative thinking, in contrast to simple problem solving. Problem solving involves an end state which is known to the thinker; the solution of the problem is a way of linking the current state of affairs to the goal state. In creative thinking the goal state is unknown; it must be constructed by the thinker.

ABSTRACTION

Abstraction is a component of theory construction that is not basically different from concept learning and rule learning. It entails identification of general features or principles from a mass of details. The principles represent classes of specific instances that differ in irrelevant details. An illustration of several levels of abstraction in the analysis of activity is shown in Figure 49. The lowest level (I) represents concrete events, as for instance an individual responding with a knee jerk when tapped on the patellar tendon. On a more abstract level (II), these events can be represented as a stimulus applied to an organism which then makes a response. Such an analysis is more general than that of Level I, and it could represent a variety of other activities. On a higher level of abstraction (III), the representation refers to activity of inanimate systems such as computers. For example, it could account for a punched card entering information into a digital computer, with printing on a teletype as the resultant activity. The Level III representation includes a wide variety of specific instances at lower levels which have a similar function in common.

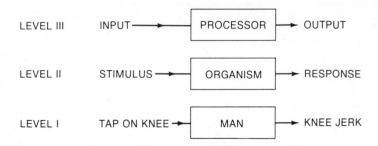

FIGURE 49   Levels of abstraction.

Since common functions can be identified in humans and computers, it is possible to conceptualize one in terms of the other. For example, human problem solving can be discussed in terms that are useful in programming computers. This approach to theorizing is similar to the informal thinking by analogy that is found in life outside the laboratory. The discovery of an analogy is an example of creative thinking and is useful in predicting new relationships.

Many analogies used are incomplete and poorly specified as to details. The more elaborate theoretical structures that result from the thinking of scientists are specified precisely, and, in sciences such as physics, they are comprehensive enough to cover large areas of knowledge. Most current theoretical formulations in psychology are more limited in scope and attempt to account for a few kinds of experiments. The term *model* is often used to designate a modest theoretical formulation devised for a limited area of application.

CONDITIONING THEORIES

One approach to learning takes conditioning experiments as the source of basic principles by which all learning can be explained. The conditioning approach views complex learning as a combination of individual conditioned units, as in the hierarchical classification of learning tasks depicted in Figure 50 (Gagné, 1964). The simplest unit of learning is assumed to be the type of relationship established in conditioning. At the next level of complexity, chaining of these units occurs, such as might be found in maze learning. Verbal learning of labels for objects is on yet another level, while concept learning involves labeling classes of objects and events at still a higher level. Beyond is rule learning, in which two or more concepts are related to one another by a rule. Finally, two or more rules may be combined into a higher-order rule in order to solve problems.

Conditioning theorists have differed in the details of their explanations of how complex behavior develops from basic conditioning relationships, but they consistently emphasize the role of stimuli and responses in

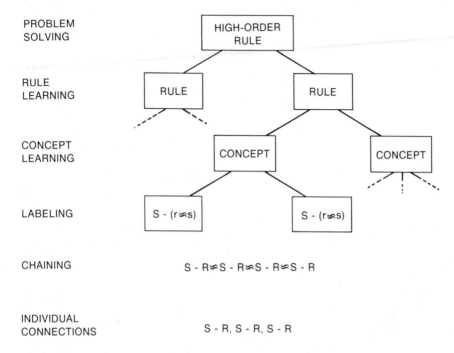

FIGURE 50   A suggested classification of types of human learning.

learning. Stimuli are changes in the environment that can be experimentally programmed for subjects; responses are actions of the subject that are observable and measurable. It is reasonable to discuss data in terms of relationships between these experimental variables.

Not all conditioning theorists agree as to the basic unit of conditioning, even though all are united in maintaining the importance of conditioning. The dominant view has been that the basic unit is composed of a stimulus associated with a response. In contrast to this response-oriented approach, an alternate interpretation states that associations may develop between stimuli. In classical conditioning a neutral stimulus is paired with an unconditioned stimulus, so the conditioning might be interpreted as an association between stimuli. When the CS is presented alone after a conditioning session, a representation of the UCS may be evoked which leads, in turn, to some appropriate response (Tolman, 1949). Many investigators hold that in order for a stimulus to become a CS it must provide information about the UCS (Rescorla, 1972). In operant experiments, auto-shaping has led investigators to consider the pigeon to be tracking a sign of a reinforcer and often responding to it as though it were the reinforcer itself (Hearst & Jenkins, 1974). Thus, not all conditioning theorists regard conditioning as a simple formation of S-R units.

INFORMATION PROCESSING

An alternative to the conditioning approach to learning is that of information processing. In the latter, the organism is assumed to process and store information, rather than acquiring habits composed of conditioned responses. Instead of explaining complex learning on the basis of principles from conditioning experiments, conditioning is explained in terms of memory of the events involved.

Figure 51 conceptualizes a classical conditioning experiment in terms of memory structure (Estes, 1973). The stimuli and responses are not arranged as an associative chain, but rather there is a hierarchical organization of representations of the events that have been learned. After sufficient conditioning trials, the organism's long-term memory has incorporated the information that a CS and a UCS occurred in some context with a specific temporal relationship. The hypothetical control elements (C_1 and C_2) represent the CS in its context and the UCS in its partially overlapping context. Activity results from interaction of present stimulation and stored memory structures such as these.

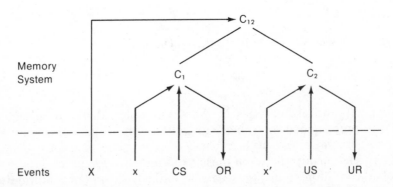

FIGURE 51 Schema representing the memory structure resulting from an effective conditioning trial. Items below the dashed line denote input and output events, including background stimulation (X) and local context (x and x'). Items above the dashed line denote control elements of the memory system and bidirectional associative connections between them.

The flow of information through the human is diagrammed in Figure 52 (Anderson & Bower, 1973). Information proceeds from the sense organs to associated storages. Next it is processed by a parser, either linguistic or perceptual. Parsers interpret the structural properties of the information and code it in terms of propositions. Propositions are the units by which memory operates, and both linguistic and nonlinguistic information is stored in propositional form. These propositions are not words, but in everyday language they correspond to ideas. A nonverbal proposition might deal with spatial relationships, as well as with facts underlying

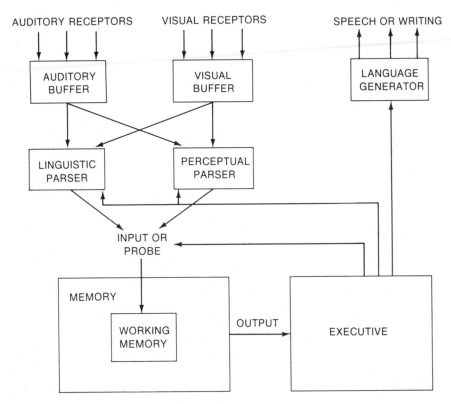

FIGURE 52   The architecture of HAM's mental system.

sentences. A visual scene or a spoken sentence could, in either case, be analyzed into a subject, predicate, and a context. For example, suppose that as one walked across a playground a boy was seen kicking a football. A structural representation is diagrammed in Figure 53, and like Estes' analysis of classical conditioning it is hierarchical in nature. The events are classified in terms of their functions and placed in a context.

Once a visual or auditory input has been placed in propositional form (parsed), a probe is made of long-term memory to find similar information stored there. When some appropriate portion of long-term memory is contacted, it is activated and is known as the working memory. There is no separate short-term store in this system; the active memory is a part of long-term memory.

A control system known as the executive determines the use of strategies, makes decisions, and directs the production of responses such as speaking. Not much can be said about the makeup of this executive system, but it is conceived as a mechanistic system and not as a little person in the head.

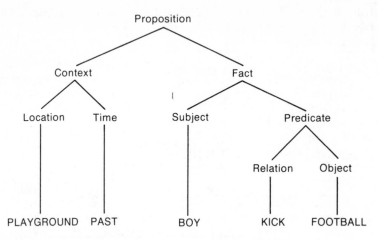

FIGURE 53   Representation of the structure of a proposition in human associative memory.

This particular information-processing system is known as HAM, for human associative memory. It was devised in order to explain the most complex human intellectual achievements, rather than the simple ones. In addition to providing an explanation for sentence memory, it aims to explain the answering of questions which may never have been heard before, and also can be applied to problem-solving behavior. Although it was designed to account for these complex human functions, it can explain simpler kinds of learning such as the rote memorization of a list of words. Words are not stored as isolated elements, but they are part of propositions including contextual components even though superficially they appear to constitute a list of unrelated words. In terms of the hierarchy of learning tasks in Figure 50, the information-processing approach starts at the top and works down to conditioning experiments. In contrast, the conditioning approach starts at the bottom and works up to problem solving.

COMPUTER SIMULATION

Information-processing theories can be tested by writing a program for a computer that will embody the relationships contained in the theory. The results of processing information by the program can then be compared with what the theorist assumed the theory would predict. With a complex theory, all of the implications cannot be known before testing of some kind has been done.

In addition to providing a technique for examining the implications of a complex theory, computer programs can themselves be considered theories. Complex human functioning can be explained by analogy with computer programs. Instead of stimulus-response units, as in condition-ing theories, the basic units are simple routines performed by the computer. At the microlevel, a state of the machine is determined by a set of switches, some on and some off. The pattern of switches that are on constitutes information, and one pattern is followed by another. A simple sequence of operations is called a subroutine, and is analogous to a short sequence of responses which the organism has learned to perform. The computer can apply tests which lead to decisions by comparing one pattern of switches with another pattern. If a discrepancy exists, a small change can be made, and another test given. This procedure can be repeated until the desired correspondence is finally obtained, at which point the decision routine stops and the program goes on to something else. A simple behavioral analogy is the pouring of water into a pail by means of a cup. The operation is repeated until a desired level is reached, perhaps by a test in which one looks at a mark on the side of the pail. When the test indicates the water has reached the mark, the pouring stops and another sequence of actions is initiated.

Hierarchical arrangements of subroutines are combined into complex programs. These subroutines are controlled by an executive program which has access to goals in the memory storage. The executive program repeatedly tests to determine whether a subgoal has been reached. An example of a computer program as a model of human processing is given in Figure 54.

Note that like the stimulus-response hierarchy of Figure 50, there are different levels of complexity. In the case of the computer analogy, this may be emphasized through the use of different languages that may be used to program a computer. It is possible to program a computer by setting sequences of individual switches in on or off positions. The status

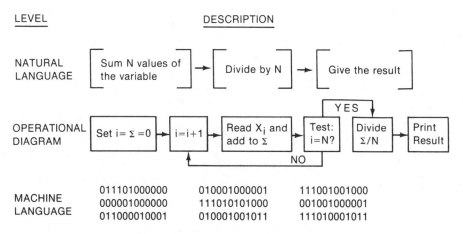

FIGURE 54 Hierarchical organization in a computer program.

of these switches is represented by a string of binary digits, in what is called machine language. Available programs also use codes amenable to human memory capacities. Instead of remembering sequences of binary alternatives, the human may code machine language into octal digits as in the coding scheme mentioned in Chapter 6. In contrast, programs exist which permit the programmer to use, as instructions, English words such as WRITE or READ, together with appropriate numerical information about where and what to read or to write. As such, a single word can stand for a substantial routine composed of many individual instructions.

Computers can be programmed to solve problems whose solutions have not been worked out. The computer has to discover something, and in a sense it is thinking. The solution of letter-series completion problems is one example (Simon & Kotovsky, 1963). A series of letters, such as the examples in Figure 55, is presented to the computer; the task is to extend the series. This kind of item appears on some tests of human intelligence, and the discovery of a way to classify the sequence is not always easy, even for college students.

```
CDCDCD__
AAABBBCCCDD__
ATBATAATBAT__
ABMCDMEFMGHM__
```

FIGURE 55　Letter-series completion problems.

When the problem is given to the computer, it draws on the information it has stored in its memory. The computer has been programmed for: knowledge of the alphabet in either a forward or reverse order; a few elementary concepts, such as "same" and "next"; a short-term memory which handles a few symbols at a time; a few simple routines to handle symbols; and the ability to proceed by trial and error to find periodicities in the sequences that repeat themselves. Once a period is found, a description of the pattern is generated, and it can be used to predict the letters that should follow in the sequence. When the computer was compared with students, it was found that the computer had difficulty with the same problems that students found difficult.

Later tests of the program uncovered some aspects of human problem solving that did not correspond in all details to that produced by the program (Kotovsky & Simon, 1973). Tests were arranged in which students had to press a lever in order to obtain a view of each element in the series. In this way the investigators sought to discover in what order humans attacked the problem. While the original program simulated humans in many respects, there were some discrepancies. Humans retained more of the information from the early stage of detection of periodicity than the computer, the latter discarding information when no longer needed. Thus, the computer program separated detection of periodicity from pattern description to a greater extent than did humans. The identification of discrepancies between program and humans can be useful in guiding alteration of the computer program and thus providing a closer simulation of human processing.

MATHEMATICAL MODELS

Mathematical models can be used by theorists of various persuasions, and mathematical models of conditioning as well as of information processing have been developed. A mathematical model consists of a set of verbal statements which incorporate one or more mathematical expressions. Two different models will be characterized briefly; one a retrieval model for short-term memory, and the other a storage model for long-term memory.

Imagine an experiment in which a subject sees a sequence of digits in a haphazard order and then judges whether a test digit was in the previous sequence (Sternberg, 1970). One of two keys is pressed to indicate the subject's decision, and the reaction time from presentation of the test digit to the press of the key is measured in thousandths of a second. With practiced subjects there are few errors, and a stable relationship is found between length of the reaction time and the size of the presentation sequence. This relationship can be represented by the equation

$$RT = a + bS.$$

In this expression, a and b are constant for a given person in a particular experiment, while that person's reaction time (RT) is slower the more digits that were presented (S). When only one digit was presented prior to the test digit, the reaction time equals a plus b. For each additional digit, another bit of time (b) is required for the judgment to be made. Thus, there are two components to the reaction time, one which stays the same no matter what the size of the set, and another which increases with size of the set. When graphed, the equation gives a straight line, as can be seen in Figure 56.

Several possible interpretations of the mathematical expression can be made, and the equation could be a part of a number of different models. For instance, one could hold that a serial search of active memory is made in order to make the judgment. This would explain why it takes longer with more items in the set. However, this suggests that it should take less time for a search in which the test digit was actually presented than for a search in which the digit was not presented. The search presumably could be stopped when the digit was found, so on the average it should take less time for the positive case than for the negative case, when S is greater than

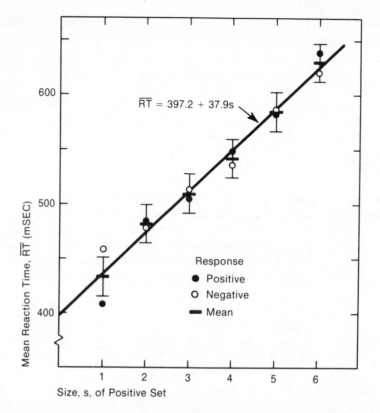

FIGURE 56 Results of an experiment on recognition of an item from active memory. The straight line was fitted by least squares to means from eight subjects.

one. The data do not support this expectation, for the constant b is the same in both the negative and positive cases, hence the slope of the function is the same in both cases. If a search is made, it is an exhaustive search and does not terminate when the digit sought is found.

An alternate interpretation holds that a parallel search of memory is made, and that after a tentative identification a check is run to make sure the judgment was correct before making a response. This check might be the component of reaction time which varies with size of the set of digits. In any case, the mathematical expression as we have described it would have to be incorporated into a larger set of statements in order to distinguish among various alternate interpretations.

In contrast to this model of retrieval time after a single presentation, consider a model of paired-associate learning over multiple trials (Atkinson, 1972). The model assumes that a given pair at any particular time is in one of three states: an unlearned state (U), a state in which the pair has been learned temporarily (T), or a state of permanent learning (P). In the unlearned state one member of a pair cannot be given in response to the other, while in the other two states a correct response can be made. A pair enters one of the two learned states during a study trial for that pair, while it can be forgotten or leave the temporary learned state on every study trial for another pair.

The mathematics in the model involves probabilities, and these probabilities remain constant for a given individual over the course of the training. The statement that a pair of associates can enter the learned state with probability of .5 means, for example, that there are five chances in ten that learning will occur on a given study trial. In any set of identical tests, learning would occur half of the time no matter what the number of occasions. An equivalent statement in a coin-tossing situation would be that a head should turn up half the time in some substantial number of tosses. The probability of a pair of associates going from one state to another on any given study trial can be represented in a transition matrix:

$$
A = \begin{array}{c} \\ P \\ T \\ U \end{array}
\begin{array}{ccc} P & T & U \\ \left[\begin{array}{ccc} 1 & 0 & 0 \\ X & 1-X & 0 \\ Y & Z & 1-Y-Z \end{array}\right] \end{array}
$$

The state of a pair at the start of a trial is represented by the rows of the matrix, while the state at the conclusion of a trial is represented by the columns. For instance, the probability of going from P to T during a study trial is 0. The probability of going from T to P is represented by X. The probability of staying in T is 1 minus the probability of the pair going from T to P. In addition to this matrix applicable to study trials, there is a probability f that a pair in T will go to U during each study trial for another pair. Thus, the longer the list of pairs, the more forgetting occurs, according to the model. By applying these equations, learning curves over successive trials can be obtained. The proportion correct on a trial will increase as in the typical learning curve.

This learning model has been applied to the learning of a second language, German, by English-speaking college students. For one group of students, the choice of pairs to study on each trial was controlled by a computer which evaluated an individual student's progress on the basis of the learning model and optimized long-term storage of the pairs. For a second group, the students themselves were permitted to choose which pairs to study on each trial. For a third group of students, the pairs were presented in a random order. Then, a week later all of the students were tested for long-term retention of the pairs. The students whose study had been supervised by the computer remembered significantly more pairs than either of the other two groups. While student selection of pairs was better than random selection, it was not as efficient as optimization by the computer on the basis of the mathematical model. The model not only provided a way of fitting curves to data from a learning experiment, but it afforded a practical application of learning principles to an instructional problem.

CONCLUDING REMARKS

Two contemporary techniques for abstracting principles out of data from learning experiments are mathematical models and computer simulation. Both are useful depending on the specific situation: mathematical models offer elegant ways of expressing simple relationships; computer simulation is useful when the relationships are quite complex.

The same view can be taken of the two general approaches, conditioning and information processing. They are not necessarily incompatible in spite of the differences in language used in the two theories. They emphasize different aspects of learning, and hence one need not be right and the other wrong. Conditioning theories focus on learning by relatively naive organisms, while information-processing approaches tend to describe activity of sophisticated organisms. The results of studies of learning to learn suggest a continuity between the learning of naive and sophisticated animals. On the other hand, complex language processing may require innate structures that are not present in animals of a simple kind. At present our understanding of these matters is incomplete. Eventually, most of the pieces may fall into place and a single comprehensive theory of learning and thinking will be formulated. For the present we are limited to calling attention to a variety of important and useful principles in each of the areas of learning that have been considered.

References

Adams, J. A., Goetz, E. T., & Marshall, P. H. Response feedback and motor learning. *Journal of Experimental Psychology,* 1972, *3,* 391–397.

Adamson, R. E., & Taylor, D. W. Functional fixedness as related to elapsed time and set. *Journal of Experimental Psychology,* 1954, *47,* 122–126.

Anderson, J. R., & Bower, G. H. *Human associative memory.* New York: Halsted Press, 1973.

Atkinson, R. C. Optimizing the learning of a second-language vocabulary. *Journal of Experimental Psychology,* 1972, *96,* 124–129.

Atkinson, R. C., & Shiffrin, R. M. The control of short-term memory. *Scientific American,* 1971, *224,* 82–90.

Azrin, N. H., & Holz, W. C. Punishment. In W. K. Honig (Ed.), *Operant behavior: Areas of research and application.* New York: Appleton-Century-Crofts, 1966.

Bach-y-Rita, P. *Brain mechanisms in sensory substitutions.* New York: Academic Press, 1972.

Baer, D. M. Laboratory control of thumb sucking by withdrawal and re-presentation of reinforcement. *Journal of the Experimental Analysis of Behavior,* 1962, *5,* 525–528.

Bahrick, H. P., & Shelly, C. Time sharing as an index of automatization. *Journal of Experimental Psychology,* 1958, *56,* 288–293.

Barnes, J. B., & Underwood, B. J. "Fate" of first-list associations in transfer theory. *Journal of Experimental Psychology,* 1959, *58,* 97–105.

Bartlett, F. *Thinking.* New York: Basic Books, 1958.

Belbin, E., Belbin, R. M., & Hill, F. A comparison between the results of three different methods of operator training. *Ergonomics,* 1957, *1,* 39–50.

Bilodeau, I. M. Information feedback. In E. A. Bilodeau (Ed.), *Principles of skill acquisition.* New York: Academic Press, 1969.

Birch, H. G., & Rabinowitz, H. S. The negative effect of previous experience upon productive thinking. *Journal of Experimental Psychology,* 1951, *41,* 121–125.

Bjork, R. A. Theoretical implications of directed forgetting. In A. W. Melton and E. Martin (Eds.), *Coding processes in human memory.* New York: Halsted Press, 1972.

Bjorkman, M., & Ottander, C. Improvement of discriminative ability by training. *Reports from the Psychological Laboratory,* University of Stockholm, 1959, No. 66.

Black, A. H. The extinction of avoidance responses under curare-like drugs. *Journal of Comparative and Physiological Psychology,* 1958, *51,* 519–524.

Bolles, R. C. Species-specific defense reactions and avoidance learning. *Psychological Review,* 1970, *77,* 32–48.

Bourne, L. E. Knowing and using concepts. *Psychological Review,* 1970, *77,* 546–556.

Bourne, L., & Archer, E. J. Time continuously on target as a function of distribution of practice. *Journal of Experimental Psychology,* 1956, *51,* 25–33.

Bourne, L. E., & Haygood, R. C. The role of stimulus redundancy in concept identification. *Journal of Experimental Psychology,* 1959, *58,* 232–238.

Bower, G. H. An association model for response and training variables in paired-associate learning. *Psychological Review,* 1962, *69,* 34–54.

Bower, G. H. Mental imagery and associative learning. In L. Gregg (Ed.), *Cognition in learning and memory.* New York: Wiley, 1972.

Bower, G. H., & Clark, M. C. Narrative stories as mediators for serial learning. *Psychonomic Science,* 1969, *14,* 181–182.

Bower, G. H., Clark, M. C., Lesgold, A. M., & Winzenz, D. Hierarchical retrieval schemes in recall of categorical word lists. *Journal of Verbal Learning and Verbal Behavior,* 1969, *8,* 323–343.

Bower, G. H., & Trabasso, T. Concept identification. In R. C. Atkinson (Ed.), *Studies in mathematical psychology.* Stanford: Stanford University Press, 1964.

Bransford, J. D., & Franks, J. J. The abstraction of linguistic ideas. *Cognitive Psychology,* 1971, *2,* 331–350.

Briggs, G. E. Acquisition, extinction, and recovery functions in retroactive inhibition. *Journal of Experimental Psychology,* 1954, *47,* 285–293.

Brown, R. Psychology and reading: Commentary on chapters 5 to 10. In H. Levin and J. P. Williams, *Basic studies on reading.* New York: Basic Books, 1970.

Brown, R., & McNeill, D. The "tip of the tongue" phenomenon. *Journal of Verbal Learning and Verbal Behavior,* 1966, *5,* 325–337.

Bruner, J. S. The course of cognitive growth. *American Psychologist,* 1964, *19,* 1–15.

Bruner, J. S., Goodnow, J. J., & Austin, G. A. *A study of thinking.* New York: Wiley, 1956.

Carlson, C. G., Hersen, M., & Eisler, R. M. Token economy programs in the treatment of hospitalized adult psychiatric patients. *The Journal of Nervous and Mental Disease,* 1972, *155,* 192–204.

Chase, R. A. An information-flow model of the organization of motor activity. I: Transduction, transmission and central control of sensory information. *Journal of Nervous and Mental Disease,* 1965, *140,* 239–251.

Cieutat, V. J., Stockwell, F. E., & Noble, C. E. The interaction of ability and amount of practice with stimulus and response meaningfulness (m, m^1) in paired-associate learning. *Journal of Experimental Psychology,* 1958, *56,* 193–202.

Collins, A. M., & Quillian, M. R. Retrieval time from semantic memory. *Journal of Verbal Learning and Verbal Behavior,* 1969, *8,* 240–247.

Conrad, R. Interference or decay over short retention intervals. *Journal of Verbal Learning and Verbal Behavior,* 1967, *6,* 49–54.

Craik, F. I. M., & Lockhart, R. S. Levels of processing: A framework for memory search. *Journal of Verbal Learning and Verbal Behavior,* 1972, *11,* 671–684.

Crossman, E. R. A theory of the acquisition of speed-skill. *Ergonomics,* 1959, *2,* 153–166.

Crovitz, H. F. Memory loci in artificial memory. *Psychonomic Science,* 1969, *16,* 182–183.

de Groot, A. D. *Thought and choice in chess.* The Hague: Mouton, 1965.

Ebbinghaus, H. *Memory.* Translated by H. A. Ruger and C. E. Bussenius. New York: Columbia University Press, 1913.

Ebenholtz, S. M. Serial learning and dimensional organization. In G. H. Bower, (Ed.) *The psychology of learning and motivation.* Vol. 5. New York: Academic Press, 1972.

Egger, M. D., & Miller, N. E. Secondary reinforcement in rats as a function of information value and reliability of the stimulus. *Journal of Experimental Psychology,* 1962, *64,* 97–104.

Eibl-Eibesfeldt, I. Concepts of ethology and their significance in the study of human behavior. In H. W. Stevenson, E. H. Hess, and H. L. Rheingold (Eds.), *Early behavior.* New York: Wiley, 1967.

Epstein, W. A further study of the influence of syntactical structure on learning. *American Journal of Psychology,* 1962, *75,* 121–126.

Epstein, W., Rock, I., & Zuckerman, C. Meaning and familiarity in associative learning. *Psychological Monographs,* 1960, *74* (Whole Number 491).

Estes, W. K. Memory and conditioning. In F. J. McGuigan and D. B. Lumsden (Eds.), *Contemporary approaches to conditioning and learning.* New York: Halsted Press, 1973.

Estes, W. K. Probability learning. In A. W. Melton (Ed.), *Categories of human learning.* New York: Academic Press, 1964.

Estes, W. K. The statistical approach to learning theory. In S. Koch (Ed.), *Psychology, a study of a science.* Vol. 2. New York: McGraw-Hill, 1959.

Estes, W. K. Transfer of verbal discriminations based on differential reward magnitudes. *Journal of Experimental Psychology,* 1966, *72,* 276–283.

Estes, W. K., & Skinner, B. F. Some quantitative properties of anxiety. *Journal of Experimental Psychology,* 1941, *29,* 390–400.

Feigenbaum, E. A., & Simon, H. A. Comment: The distinctiveness of stimuli. *Psychological Review,* 1961, *68,* 285–288.

Findlay, A. *A hundred years of chemistry.* (2nd ed.) London: Duckworth, 1948.

Fitts, P. M. Perceptual-motor skill learning. In A. W. Melton (Ed.), *Categories of human learning.* New York: Academic Press, 1964.

Fleishman, E. A., & Hempel, W. E., Jr. Changes in factor structure of a complex psychomotor test as a function of practice. *Psychometrika,* 1954, *19,* 239–252.

Freedman, J. L., & Landauer, T. K. Retrieval of long-term memory: "Tip-of-the-tongue" phenomenon. *Psychonomic Science,* 1966, *4,* 309–310.

Gagné, R. M. Problem solving. In A. W. Melton (Ed.), *Categories of human learning.* New York: Academic Press, 1964.

Gagné, R. M., & Gibson, J. J. Research in the recognition of aircraft. In J. J. Gibson (Ed.), *Motion Picture Training and Research.* (Army Air Force Aviation Psychology Program, Research Reports, Rep. No. 7) Washington, D.C.: United States Government Printing Office, 1947.

Gardner, R. A., & Gardner, B. T. Teaching sign language to a chimpanzee. *Science,* 1969, *165,* 664–672.

Gelman, R. Conservation acquisition: A problem of learning to attend to relevant attributes. *Journal of Experimental Child Psychology,* 1969, *2,* 167–187.

Gibson, E. J. *Principles of perceptual learning and development.* New York: Appleton-Century-Crofts, 1969.

Gibson, J. J., & Gibson, E. J. Perceptual learning: Differentiation or enrichment? *Psychological Review,* 1955, *62,* 32–41.

Glucksberg, S., & Weisberg, R. W. Verbal behavior and problem solving: Some effects of labeling in a functional fixedness problem. *Journal of Experimental Psychology,* 1966, *71,* 659–664.

Greeno, J. G. The structure of memory and the process of solving problems. In R. L. Solso (Ed.), *Contemporary issues in cognitive psychology: The Loyola Symposium.* New York: Halsted Press, 1972.

Harlow, H. F. The formation of learning sets. *Psychological Review,* 1949, *56,* 51–65.

Harris, F. R., Wolf, M. M., & Baer, D. M. Effects of adult social reinforcement on child behavior. *Young Children,* 1964, *20,* 8–17.

Hartman, T. F., & Grant, D. A. Effect of intermittent reinforcement on acquisition, extinction, and spontaneous recovery of the conditioned eyelid response. *Journal of Experimental Psychology,* 1960, *60,* 89–96.

Hayes, J. R. Memory, goals, and problem solving. In B. Kleinmutz (Ed.), *Problem solving: Research, method, and theory.* New York: Wiley, 1966.

Hearst, E., & Jenkins, H. M. *Sign-tracking: The stimulus-reinforcer relation and directed action.* Austin, Texas: Psychonomic Society, 1974.

Hefferline, R. F., Keenan, B., & Harford, R. A. Escape and avoidance conditioning in human subjects without their observation of the response. *Science,* 1959, *130,* 1338–1339.

Hingten, J. N., & Trost, F. C., Jr. Shaping cooperative responses in early childhood schizophrenics: II Reinforcement of mutual physical contact and vocal responses. In R. Ulrich, T. Stachnik, and J. Mabry (Eds.), *Control of human behavior.* Vol. 1. Glenview, Ill.: Scott, Foresman, 1966.

Hockey, R. Rate of presentation in running memory and direct manipulation of in-put processing strategies. *Quarterly Journal of Psychology,* 1973, *25,* 104–111.

Hull, C. L. *Principles of behavior.* New York: Appleton-Century-Crofts, 1943.

Hull, C. L. *A behavior system: An introduction to behavior theory concerning the individual organism.* New Haven: Yale University Press, 1952.

Johnson, N. F. The psychological reality of phrase-structure rules. *Journal of Verbal Learning and Verbal Behavior,* 1965, *4,* 469–475.

Johnson, R. B. More on "bizarre images in artificial memory." *Psychonomic Science,* 1972, *26,* 101–102.

Jung, J. Effects of response meaningfulness (m) on transfer of training under two different paradigms. *Journal of Experimental Psychology,* 1963, *65,* 377–384.

Kahneman, D., & Tversky, A. On the psychology of prediction. *Psychological Review,* 1973, *80,* 237–251.

Kareev, Y. *A model of human game playing.* (Tech. Rep. No. 36) San Diego: University of California, Center for Human Information Processing, 1973.

Katkin, E. S., & Murray, E. N. Instrumental conditioning of autonomically mediated behavior. *Psychological Bulletin,* 1968, *70,* 52–68.

Kay, H. The development of motor skills from birth to adolescence. In E. Bilodeau (Ed.), *Principles of skill acquisition.* New York: Academic Press, 1969.

Keele, S. W. *Attention and human performance.* Pacific Palisades: Goodyear, 1973.

Keesey, R. R. Intracranial reward delay and the acquisition of a brightness discrimination. *Science,* 1964, *143,* 702–703.

Kendler, H. H., & Kendler, T. S. Vertical and horizontal processes in problem solving. *Psychological Review,* 1962, *69,* 1–16.

Keppel, G., & Underwood, B. J. Proactive inhibition in short-term retention of single items. *Journal of Verbal Learning and Verbal Behavior,* 1962, *1,* 153–161.

Kimble, G. A., & Reynolds, B. Eyelid conditioning as a function of the interval between conditioned and unconditioned stimuli. In G. A. Kimble (Ed.), *Foundations of conditioning and learning.* New York: Appleton-Century-Crofts, 1967.

Kinchla, R. A. Selective processes in sensory memory: A probe-comparison procedure. In S. Kornblum (Ed.), *Attention and performance IV.* New York: Academic Press, 1973.

Kotovsky, K., & Simon, H. A. Empirical tests of a theory of human acquisition of concepts for sequential patterns. *Cognitive Psychology,* 1973, *4,* 339–424.

Kreuger, W. C. F. The effect of overlearning on retention. *Journal of Experimental Psychology,* 1929, *12,* 71–78.

Lashley, K. An examination of the continuity theory as applied to discrimination learning. *Journal of General Psychology,* 1942, *26,* 241–265.

Lawson, E. A note on the influence of different orders of approximation to the English language upon eye-voice span. *Quarterly Journal of Experimental Psychology,* 1961, *13,* 53–55.

Lazlo, J. Training of fast tapping with reduction of kinaesthetic, tactile, visual, and auditory sensations. *Quarterly Journal of Experimental Psychology,* 1967, *19,* 344–349.

Lazlo, J. I., & Baguley, R. A. Motor memory and bilateral transfer. *Journal of Motor Behavior,* 1971, *3,* 235–240.

Lazlo, J. I., & Bairstow, P. J. Accuracy of movement, peripheral feedback, and efference copy. *Journal of Motor Behavior,* 1971, *3,* 241–252.

Levine, M. Cue neutralization: The effect of random reinforcements upon discrimination learning. *Journal of Experimental Psychology,* 1962, *63,* 438–443.

Levine, M. Hypothesis theory and nonlearning despite ideal S-R reinforcement contingencies. *Psychological Review,* 1971, *78,* 130–140.

Mackworth, J. F. Performance decrement in vigilance, threshold, and high speed perceptual-motor tasks. *Canadian Journal of Psychology,* 1964, *18,* 209–223.

Martin, E. Transfer of verbal paired associates. *Psychological Review,* 1965, *72,* 327–343.

McCrary, J. W., & Hunter, W. S. Serial position curves in verbal learning. *Science,* 1953, *117,* 131–134.

McGuire, W. J. A multi-process model for paired-associate learning. *Journal of Experimental Psychology,* 1961, *62,* 335–347.

Melton, A. W. Implications of short-term memory for a general theory of memory. *Journal of Verbal Learning and Verbal Behavior,* 1963, *2,* 1–21.

Meyer, D. R., LoPopolo, M. H., & Singh, D. Learning and transfer in the monkey as a function of differential levels of incentive. *Journal of Experimental Psychology,* 1966, *72,* 284–286.

Miller, G. A. The magical number seven, plus or minus two: Some limits on our capacity for processing information. *Psychological Review,* 1956, *63,* 81–97.

Miller, N. E. Experiments on motivation: Studies combining psychological, physiological, and pharmacological techniques. *Science,* 1957, *126,* 1271–1278.

Miller, N. Learning of visceral and glandular responses. *Science,* 1969, *163,* 434–445.

Miller, N. E. Liberalization of basic S-R concepts: Extension to conflict behavior, motivation, and social learning. In S. Koch (Ed.), *Psychology: A study of a science.* Vol. 2. New York: McGraw-Hill, 1959.

Miller, N. E. Some reflections on the law of effect produce a new alternative to drive reduction. In M. R. Jones (Ed.), *Nebraska symposium on motivation,* 1963. Lincoln: University of Nebraska Press, 1963.

Miller, N. E., & Dollard, J. *Social learning and imitation.* New Haven: Yale University Press, 1941.

Millward, R. B., & Spoehr, K. T. The direct measurement of hypothesis sampling strategies. *Cognitive Psychology,* 1973, *4,* 1–38.

Montague, W. E. Elaborative strategies in verbal learning and memory. In G. H. Bower (Ed.), *The psychology of learning and motivation.* Vol. 6. New York: Academic Press, 1972.

Murdock, B. B., Jr. The retention of individual items. *Journal of Experimental Psychology,* 1961, *62,* 618–625.

Murdock, B. B., Jr., & Walker, K. D. Modality effects in free recall. *Journal of Verbal Learning and Verbal Behavior,* 1969, *8,* 665–676.

Neimark, E., & Saltzman, I. J. Intentional and incidental learning with different rates of stimulus presentation. *American Journal of Psychology,* 1953, *66,* 618–621.

Newell, A., Shaw, J. C., & Simon, H. A. Elements of a theory of human problem solving. *Psychological Review,* 1958, *65,* 151–169.

Newell, A., & Simon, H. A. *Human problem solving.* Englewood Cliffs, New Jersey: Prentice-Hall, 1972.

Noble, C. E. An analysis of meaning. *Psychological Review,* 1952, *59,* 421–430.

Notterman, J. M., Schoenfeld, W. N., & Bersh, P. J. Conditioned heart-rate response in human beings during experimental anxiety. *Journal of Comparative and Physiological Psychology*, 1952, *45*, 1–8.

O'Bryan, K. G., and Boersma, F. J. Eye movements, perceptual activity, and conservation development. *Journal of Experimental Child Psychology*, 1971, *12*, 157–169.

Olds, J. A., & Milner, P. Positive reinforcement produced by electrical stimulation of septal areas and other regions of rat brain. *Journal of Comparative and Physiological Psychology*, 1954, *47*, 419–427.

Olson, D. R. *Cognitive development of the child's acquisition of diagonality*. New York: Academic Press, 1970.

Osgood, C. E. Motivational dynamics of language behavior. In M. R. Jones (Ed.), *Nebraska symposium on motivation*, 1957. Lincoln: University of Nebraska Press, 1957.

Paivio, A. *Imagery and verbal processes*. New York: Holt, Rinehart & Winston, 1971.

Paivio, A., Yuille, J. C., & Madigan, S. Concreteness, imagery, and meaningfulness values for 925 nouns. *Journal of Experimental Psychology Monograph Supplement*, 1968, *76*, (1, Part 2).

Pavlov, I. P. *Lectures on conditioned reflexes*. Translated by W. H. Gantt. New York: International, 1928.

Peterson, L. Concurrent verbal activity. *Psychological Review*, 1969, *76*, 376–386.

Peterson, L. R., & James, L. H. Successive tests of short-term retention. *Psychonomic Science*, 1967, *8*, 423–424.

Peterson, L. R., & Johnson, S. T. Some effects of minimizing articulation on short-term retention. *Journal of Verbal Learning and Verbal Behavior*, 1971, *10*, 346–354.

Peterson, L. R., & Peterson, M. J. Short-term retention of individual verbal items. *Journal of Experimental Psychology*, 1959, *58*, 193–198.

Pew, R. W. Acquisition of hierarchical control over the temporal organization of a skill. *Journal of Experimental Psychology*, 1966, *71*, 764–771.

Pfaffmann, C. Taste, its sensory and motivating properties. *American Scientist*, 1964, *52*, 187–206.

Poincare, H. Mathematical creation. In P. E. Vernon (Ed.), *Creativity*. Baltimore: Penguin, 1970.

Pollack, I., & Pickett, J. M. The intelligibility of excerpts from conversational speech. *Language and Speech*, 1963, *6*, 165–171.

Posner, M. I. Rate of presentation and order of recall in immediate memory. *British Journal of Psychology*, 1964, *55*, 303–307.

Postman, L. Organization and interference. *Psychological Review*, 1971, *78*, 290–302.

Postman, L. Short-term memory and incidental learning. In A. W. Melton (Ed.), *Categories of human learning.* New York: Academic Press, 1964.

Postman, L. Transfer of training as a function of experimental paradigms and degree of first-list learning. *Journal of Verbal Learning and Verbal Behavior,* 1962, *1,* 109–118.

Postman, L., & Phillips, L. W. Short-term temporal changes in free recall. *Quarterly Journal of Experimental Psychology,* 1965, *17,* 132–138.

Postman, L., & Stark, K. The role of response availability in transfer and interference. *Journal of Experimental Psychology,* 1969, *79,* 168–177.

Premack, D. Reinforcement theory. In M. R. Jones (Ed.), *Nebraska symposium on motivation,* 1965. Lincoln: University of Nebraska Press, 1965.

Premack, D. Language in chimpanzee? *Science,* 1971, *172,* 808–822.

Pronko, N. H. On learning to play the violin at the age of four without tears. *Psychology Today,* 1969, *2,* 52.

Rachman, S., & Teasdale, J. *Aversion therapy and behavior disorder; an analysis.* London: Routledge and Kegan Paul, 1969.

Rawlings, E. I., Rawlings, I. L., Cheu, S. S., & Yilk, M. D. The facilitating effects of mental rehearsal in the acquisition of rotary pursuit tracking. *Psychonomic Science,* 1972, *26,* 71–73.

Razran, G. H. A quantitative study of meaning by a conditioned salivary technique (semantic conditioning). *Science,* 1939, *90,* 89–90.

Reitman, J. S. Mechanisms of forgetting in short-term memory. *Cognitive Psychology,* 1971, *2,* 185–195.

Reitman, W. R. *Cognition and thought.* New York: Wiley, 1965.

Rescorla, R. A. Informational variables in Pavlovian conditioning. In G. H. Bower (Ed.), *The psychology of learning and motivation.* Vol. 6. New York: Academic Press, 1972.

Restle, F. The selection of strategies in cue learning. *Psychological Review,* 1962, *69,* 11–19.

Restle, F., & Brown, E. Organization of serial pattern learning. In G. H. Bower (Ed.), *The psychology of learning and motivation.* Vol. 4. New York: Academic Press, 1970.

Ricciuti, H. N. Object grouping and selective ordering behavior in infants 12 to 24 months old. *Merrill-Palmer Quarterly,* 1965, *11,* 129–148.

Rock, I. The role of repetition in associative learning. *American Journal of Psychology,* 1957, *70,* 186–193.

Rosenberg, S., & Schiller, W. J. Semantic coding and incidental sentence recall. *Journal of Experimental Psychology,* 1971, *90,* 345–346.

Rundus, D., & Atkinson, R. C. Rehearsal processes in free recall: A procedure for direct observation. *Journal of Verbal Learning and Verbal Behavior,* 1970, *9,* 99–105.

Sachs, J. S. Recognition memory for syntactic and semantic aspects of connected discourse. *Perception & Psychophysics,* 1967, *2,* 437–442.

Schneiderman, N., Fuentes, I., & Gormezano, I. Acquisition and extinction of the classically conditioned eyelid response in the albino rabbit. *Science,* 1962, *136,* 650–652.

Seligman, M. E. P., Maier, S. F., & Solomon, R. L. Unpredictable and uncontrollable events. In F. R. Brush (Ed.), *Aversive conditioning and learning.* New York: Academic Press, 1969.

Sheffield, F. D., & Roby, T. B. Reward value of a nonnutritive sweet taste. *Journal of Comparative and Physiological Psychology,* 1950, *43,* 471–481.

Shiffrin, R. M. Information persistence in short-term memory. *Journal of Experimental Psychology,* 1973, *100,* 39–49.

Simon, H. A., & Kotovsky, K. Human acquisition of concepts for sequential patterns. *Psychological Review,* 1963, *70,* 534–546.

Skinner, B. F. *Science and human behavior.* New York: Macmillan, 1953.

Snoddy, G. S. Learning and stability. *Journal of Applied Psychology,* 1926, *10,* 1–36.

Solomon, R. L. Punishment. *American Psychologist,* 1964, *19,* 239–253.

Spence, K. W. Cognitive and drive factors in the extinction of the conditioned eye blink in human subjects. *Psychological Review,* 1966, *73,* 445–458.

Spence, K. W. The differential response in animals to stimuli varying within a single dimension. *Psychological Review,* 1937, *44,* 430–444.

Sperling, G. A model for visual memory tasks. *Human Factors,* 1963, *5,* 19–30.

Sperling, S. Reversal learning and resistance to extinction: A review of the rat literature. *Psychological Bulletin,* 1965, *63,* 281–297.

Spielberger, C. D., & DeNike, L. D. Descriptive behaviorism versus cognitive theory in verbal operant conditioning. *Psychological Review,* 1966, *73,* 306–326.

Sternberg, S. Memory-scanning: Mental processes revealed by reaction-time experiments. In J. S. Antrobus (Ed.), *Cognition and affect.* New York: Little, Brown, 1970.

Taylor, J. A. The relationship of anxiety to the conditioned eyelid response. *Journal of Experimental Psychology,* 1951, *41,* 81–92.

Terrace, H. S. Wavelength generalization after discrimination with and without errors. *Science,* 1964, *144,* 61–63.

Tolman, E. C. Cognitive maps in rats and men. *Psychological Review,* 1948, *55,* 189–208.

Tolman, E. C. There is more than one kind of learning. *Psychological Review,* 1949, *56,* 144–155.

Tulving, E. Episodic and semantic memory. In E. Tulving and W. Donaldson (Eds.), *Organization of memory*. New York: Academic Press, 1972.

Tulving, E. Subjective organization in free recall of unrelated words. *Psychological Review*, 1962, *69*, 344–354.

Tulving, E. Subjective organization and effects of repetition in multi-trial free-recall learning. *Journal of Verbal Learning and Verbal Behavior*, 1966, *5*, 193–199.

Ulich, E. Some experiments on the function of mental training in the acquisition of motor skills. *Ergonomics*, 1967, *10*, 411–419.

Underwood, B. J. Interference and forgetting. *Psychological Review*, 1957, *64*, 49–60.

Underwood, B. J. Proactive inhibition with increased recall time. *American Journal of Psychology*, 1950, *63*, 594–599.

Underwood, B. J. Speed of learning and amount retained: A consideration of methodology. *Psychological Bulletin*, 1954, *51*, 276–282.

Underwood, B. J., Rehula, R., & Keppel, G. Item-selection in paired-associate learning. *American Journal of Psychology*, 1962, *75*, 353–371.

Watson, J. B. *Behaviorism*. Chicago: The University of Chicago Press, 1930.

Waugh, N. C., & Norman, D. A. Primary memory. *Psychological Review*, 1965, *72*, 89–104.

Welford, A. T. *Fundamentals of skill*. London: Methuen, 1968.

Wickens, D. D. Characteristics of word encoding. In A. W. Melton and E. Martin (Eds.), *Coding processes in human memory*. New York: Halsted Press, 1972.

Williams, D. R., & Williams, H. Auto-maintenance in the pigeon: Sustained pecking despite contingent nonreinforcement. *Journal of the Experimental Analysis of Behavior*. 1969, *12*, 511–520.

Wollen, K. A., Weber, A., & Lowry, D. H. Bizarreness versus interaction of mental images as determinants of learning. *Cognitive Psychology*, 1972, *3*, 518–523.

Young, R. K. Tests of three hypotheses about the effective stimulus in serial learning. *Journal of Experimental Psychology*, 1962, *63*, 307–313.

Zeaman, D., & House, B. J. The role of attention in retardate discrimination learning. In N. Ellis (Ed.), *Handbook of mental deficiency*. New York: McGraw-Hill, 1963.

Name Index

Adams, J. A., 87, 89
Adamson, R. E., 102
Anderson, J. R., 110–111
Archer, E. J., 93
Atkinson, R. C., 63, 116–117
Austin, G. A., 101
Azrin, N. H., 18

Bach-y-Rita, P., 45
Baer, D. M., 22
Baguley, R. A., 89
Bahrick, H. P., 82
Bairstow, P. J., 87
Barnes, J. B., 72
Belbin, E., 80
Belbin, R. M., 80
Bersh, P. J., 11
Birch, H. G., 76, 102
Bjork, R. A., 69
Bjorkman, M., 42
Black, A. H., 27
Boersma, F. J., 98
Bolles, R. C., 20
Bourne, L. E., 41, 93, 98–99
Bower, G. H., 35, 49, 51–52, 75–76,
    110–111
Bransford, J. D., 66–67
Briggs, G. E., 71
Brown, R., 45, 91
Bruner, J. S., 96, 98, 101

Carlson, C. G., 22
Chase, R. A., 80, 87
Cieutat, V. J., 47–48
Clark, M. C., 51–52, 75–76
Collins, A. M., 67
Crossman, E. R., 83–84
Crovitz, H. F., 59

de Groot, A. D., 105
De Nike, L. D., 29
Dollard, J., 43

Ebenholtz, S. M., 57
Egger, M. D., 29
Eibl-Eibesfeldt, I., 1
Eisler, R. M., 22
Epstein, W., 49, 58
Estes, W. K., 20, 29, 110, 111

Fitts, P. M., 79
Fleishman, E. A., 80
Franks, J. J., 66–67

Freedman, J. L., 73
Fuentes, I., 4–5

Gagné, R. M., 42–43, 108
Gardner, R. A., 95
Gardner, B. T., 95
Gelman, R., 98
Gibson, E. J., 42–43, 76
Gibson, J. J., 42
Glucksberg, S., 102
Goetz, E. T., 87, 89
Goodnow, J. J., 101
Gormezano, I., 4–5
Grant, D. A., 7
Greeno, J. G., 100

Harford, R. A., 29–30
Harlow, H. F., 35
Harris, F. R., 22
Hartman, T. F., 7
Hayes, J. R., 103–104
Haygood, R. C., 41
Hearst, E., 109
Hefferline, R. F., 29–30
Hempel, W. E., Jr., 80
Hersen, M., 22
Hill, F., 80
Hingten, J. N., 21–22
Hockey, R., 77
Holz, W. C., 18
House, B. J., 40–41
Hull, C. L., 25, 26, 29
Hunter, W. S., 58

James, L. H., 74
Jenkins, H. M., 109
Johnson, N. F., 58
Johnson, R. B., 59
Johnson, S. T., 63
Jung, J., 57

Kahneman, D., 80
Kareev, Y., 106
Katkin, E. S., 21
Kay, H., 85–86
Keele, S. W., 90
Keenan, B., 30
Kendler, H. H., 39
Kendler, T. S., 39
Keppel, G., 53–54, 74, 77–78
Kimble, G. A., 6
Kinchla, R. A., 66
Kotovsky, K., 114–115

Landauer, T. K., 73
Lashley, K., 34
Lazlo, J. I., 87, 89, 90
Lesgold, A. M., 51–52
Levine, M., 100
LoPopolo, M. H., 29
Lowry, D. H., 49

Mackworth, J. F., 94
Madigan, S., 48
Maier, S. F., 19
Marshall, P. H., 87, 89
McCrary, J. W., 58
McGuire, W. J., 55
Meyer, D. R., 29
Miller, G. A., 64
Miller, N., 21, 25, 26, 29, 43
Millward, R. B., 100
Milner, P., 25–26
Montague, W. E., 53
Murdock, B. B., Jr., 63, 66
Murray, E. N., 21

Neimark, E., 69
Newell, A., 104
Noble, C. E., 47–48
Norman, D. A., 62
Notterman, J. M., 11

O'Bryan, K. G., 98
Olds, J. A., 25–26
Olson, D. R., 98
Ottander, C., 42

Paivio, A., 48, 49
Pavlov, I., 3–4, 7, 9
Peterson, L. R., 60, 63, 66, 74, 83
Peterson, M. J., 60
Pew, R. W., 90
Pfaffman, C., 25
Phillips, L. W., 65
Pickett, J. M., 44
Pollack, I., 44
Posner, M. I., 76
Postman, L., 56, 65, 68, 73
Premack, D., 26, 96
Pronko, N. H., 90

Quillian, M. R., 67

Rabinowitz, H. S., 102
Rachman, S., 23
Rawlings, E. I., 80
Rawlings, I. L., 80
Razran, G. H., 9

Rehula, R., 53–54
Reitman, W. R., 78
Rescorla, R. A., 109
Restle, F., 91, 100
Reynolds, B., 6
Ricciuti, H. N., 97
Roby, T. B., 25
Rock, I., 49, 53
Rosenberg, S., 69
Rundus, D., 63

Sachs, J. S., 66
Saltzman, I. J., 69
Schiller, W. J., 69
Schneiderman, N., 4–5
Seligman, M. E. P., 19
Sheffield, F. D., 25
Shelly, C., 82
Shiffrin, R. M., 78
Shoenfeld, W. N., 11
Simon, H. A., 104, 114–115
Singh, D., 29
Skinner, B. F., 13, 15, 20, 24
Snoddy, G. S., 84
Solomon, R. L., 19
Spence, K. W., 11, 31, 32, 34
Sperling, G. A., 62
Sperling, S., 35
Spielberger, C. D., 29
Spoehr, K. T., 100
Stark, K., 73
Sternberg, S., 115–116
Stockwell, F. E., 47–48

Taylor, J. A., 10, 102
Teasdale, J., 23
Terrace, H. S., 33
Tolman, E. C., 109
Trabasso, T., 35
Trost, F. C., Jr., 21–22
Tulving, E., 49, 50–51, 68

Ulich, E., 80
Underwood, B. J., 53–54, 72, 74, 75, 76, 77–78

Walker, K. D., 63
Watson, J. B., 5
Waugh, N. C., 62
Weber, A., 49
Weisberg, R. W., 102
Welford, A. T., 91, 94
Wickens, D. D., 74
Williams, D. R., 27–28, 76
Williams, H., 27–28, 76
Winzenz, D., 51–52

Wolf, M. M., 22
Wollen, K. A., 49

Yilk, M. D., 80

Young, R. K., 57
Yuille, J. C., 48

Zeaman, D., 40–41
Zuckerman, C., 49

Subject Index

Acquisition of skill: early stage, 79–80; improvement, 84–87; intermediate stage, 80–81; late stage, 82; limit to skill, 83; in playing games, 105; practice of part or whole, 94; rest intervals during practice, 93
Activity rate, 26, 30
Anticipation, 4; and incentive motivation, 28, 29; responses, 29; in serial learning, 47
Associative stage of discrimination learning, 40, 41
Attribute identification, 97–98
Autonomic responses, 20, 21
Auto-shaping, 27, 28, 109
Avoidance training, 19, 20, 23

Backward conditioning, 7
Backward strategy, 104
Behavior: animal, 2, 29; chains, 17; conditioning principles, 12; effect of emotion on, 20; extinction, 16; human, 2; influence of drugs on, 15; insightful, 38; instinctive, 1; modification of, 30; reinforcement, 24, 28–30; token economies, 22
Bilateral transfer, 89
Blind persons and sensory substitution, 45

Chaining, 14, 17
Classical conditioning, 3, 4, 14, 18, 20, 23, 29; of animals, 4, 109; basis for learning, 10; and conditioned anxiety, 20; importance of, 12; influencing response patterns, 5; interstimulus interval, 5, 7; measuring responses, 5; opposed to instrumental, 14; punishment, 18; semantic generalization, 9
Closed-loop analysis, 87, 88
Coding, 43, 44, 55, 56, 64, 96
Computer simulation, 112–115, 118

Concept identification, 41, 100, 101
Conditioned anxiety, 20
Conditioned helplessness, 19
Conditioned response (CR), 3, 7–9, 11, 72
Conditioned stimulus, 3, 7–9, 11
Conditioned suppression, 20
Conditioning: and learning, 12, 110; rate of, 9; reporting, 30; second-order, 9; semantic generalization, 9; stimulus-response interpretation, 11; stimulus-stimulus interpretation, 11; techniques in treating behavior problems, 21; theories, 108, 113; trials, 31
Conjunction, 98
Conservative focusing, 101, 102
Continuity interpretation, 31–34

Delay conditioning, 7
Dimensional shift, 38–40
Discrimination, 9, 12, 17, 31–40; and language behavior, 96, 97; learning, 31–42; object, 35–37; reversals, 37–39
Disjunction, 98
Drive-reduction theory, 25, 26, 30
Drop-out technique, 53

Escape training, 19
Excitation, 31, 32
Executive, 111
Extinction: of conditioned response, 7, 9, 11, 12, 31; latent, 27; one-trial, 38; of undesirable behavior, 16

Feedback: augmented, 86–89, 92; intrinsic, 86–89; with motor programs, 90
Fixed-interval (FI) schedule, 15
Fixed problems, 104
Fixed-ratio (FR) schedule, 15
Focus gambling, 101, 102

Forgetting, 69–76
Forward strategy, 104
Free recall learning, 46, 49, 52, 63
Functional fixedness, 102

Galvanic skin response, 5, 21
Game playing, 104, 105
General transfer, 55
Generalization, 12, 17; gradient, 31–34; semantic, 9
Grammatical structure, 58

Hierarchical organization, 51, 52, 66, 91, 92
Human associative memory (HAM), 112
Hypothesis testing, 41, 100, 101, 104

Incidental learning, 68, 69
Information processing, 61, 68, 69, 112–118; and coding, 64; and rehearsal, 63, 64, 66, 70, 77
Inhibition, 31, 32
Instinctive behavior, 1, 2
Instructed learning, 18, 69
Instrumental conditioning, 13, 15, 16, 20, 21, 23, 29; and chaining, 14; and conditioned anxiety, 20; discrimination in, 17; generalization in, 17; and operant conditioning, 13, 86; and punishment, 18; techniques of, 96; and voluntary control, 21
Interactive problems, 104
Internal standard, 87–90
Interstimulus interval, 5, 6

Labels: and binary-digit sequences, 64; and classification for objects, 96; and coding responses, 43, 44, 99; and transfer effects, 55, 56; and verbal learning, 55, 102, 108
Latent extinction, 27
Latent learning, 27, 28, 30
Learning, 1–3, 12; concept, 96, 97, 99, 108; curves, 32–36; discrimination, 31–42; and free recall, 46, 49, 52, 63; incidental, 68, 69; instructed, 18, 69; latent, 27; paired-associate, 46, 47, 52–55, 57, 81, 103; perceptual, 42–44, 55; perceptual-motor, 79, 80, 91; and performance, 30; reinforcement, 26; response, 54; rule, 98, 108; serial, 46, 57–59; stimulus, 55; theories, 34–36, 40–41; verbal, 55, 72, 102, 108

Mathematical models, 115
Memory: decay of, 76–78; episodic, 68; long-term, 61, 66; semantic, 66; sensory, 61, 62, 66; working, 61, 63, 64, 66
Motivation, 28; deprivation, 28; incentive, 28, 29; in skill improvement, 30, 84
Motor programs, 90

Need-reduction theory, 25
Negative transfer, 50, 56
Noncontinuity interpretation, 34, 35
Nonreversal shift, 39, 40

Operant conditioning, 13, 17
Overtraining, 35

Paired-associate learning, 46, 47, 52–55, 57, 81, 103
Parsers, 110
Partial reinforcement, 7, 15–16
Peak shift, 32, 33
Perception, 44
Perceptual learning, 42–44, 55
Perceptual-motor learning, 79, 80, 91
Performance, 26, 28, 30, 84; automatic, 82; motor and feedback, 86, 89; skilled, 79; variations in, 86
Positive transfer, 50, 56
Proactive interference, 74–76, 78
Problem solving, 34, 99, 100, 102; by computers, 114; and concept identification, 100, 101; game playing as a kind of, 104; human, 108, 114; hypothesis testing, 41, 100, 101, 104; by monkeys, 35, 36; strategies of, 101, 104; subgoals in, 103, 104, 106–107
Progressive deepening, 105
Progressive-part method, 94
Propositions, 110–112
Psychosomatic illness, 21
Punishment, 18, 19, 22, 24

Reflex, 1, 2
Reinforcement, 7–9, 14–16, 86; chaining, 14; and drive reduction, 24; and extinction, 16; and illness, 21; influencing behavior by, 28–30; learning, 26; reinforced and nonreinforced trials, 7–9; schedules, 15; shaping, 14; through social interaction, 23; in treating behavior problems, 21–22

Reinforcers: negative, 24; positive, 24; primary, 16–17; secondary, 17
Representation: animal, 95; human, 96
Response: as actions, 109; autonomic, 20; conditioned, 3, 7–9, 11, 72; extinction, 16; learning, 54; measuring, 5; patterns, 5; shaping, 14; types, 5; unconditioned, 3, 11
Rest intervals, 93
Retarded children and discrimination learning, 40, 41
Retention interval, 60, 70
Retroactive interference, 70–72, 76
Reversal shift, 39, 40
Rewards, 13, 21, 22, 28, 29, 38
Rule learning, 98, 108

Selection stage of discrimination learning, 40, 41
Selective attention, 40, 41
Sensory substitution, 45
Serial learning, 46, 57–59
Shaping, 14, 21
Skills, 2; reading, 44; serial learning, 57
Specific transfer, 55
Spontaneous recovery of conditioned response, 7, 72
Stimulation, offset and onset, 25, 26, 30
Stimulus, 31, 109; aversive, 18, 19, 25; coding responses to, 43; dis-criminative, 17; drives, 25–26; reinforcing, 7; response to, 33, 34; in serial learning, 57
Stimulus learning, 55
Stimulus-response relationship, 3, 31–34, 39, 40, 91
Strategies, 101, 104
Subjective organization, 49, 51
Summation theory, 32–34
Suzuki method, 89, 90
Symbols: verbal, 96–97; visual, 96

Taylor Manifest Anxiety Scale, 10
Temporal conditioning, 7
Tests: free recall, 72–74; multiple-choice, 72, 73; Taylor Manifest Anxiety Scale, 10
Thinking: and computers, 114; in problem solving, 104–105; as a skill, 95; and verbal symbols, 96
Token economies, 22
Trace conditioning, 7
Transitional error probability, 58
Transposition, 33, 34

Unconditioned response (UCR), 3, 11
Unconditioned stimulus, 3, 7, 11

Variable-interval (VI) schedule, 15
Variable-ratio (VR) schedule, 15
Verbal learning, 55, 72, 102, 108
Voluntary responses, 20, 21

2 3 4 5 6 7 8 9 10 –CP– 80 79 78 77 76 75